Contents

Unit	Language	Skills: Pupils' Book	Skills: Activity Book
Welcome! p4	Greetings Present simple		
1 Getting ready p6	Present simple Present continuous Adverbs of manner	Reading: A personal description (family, routine) Listening: Write down telephone numbers. Speaking: Make arrangements.	Listening: Identify if statements about a picture are true or false. Writing: Punctuation. Write a personal description.
Music p14 Music around the world	*(Bagpipes) are (old instruments).* *(They) sing and wear (masks and hats).*	Project: Make a leaflet about music in your country.	
2 The storm p16	*was/were/wasn't/weren't* Past simple regular (affirmative, negative and questions)	R: A diary entry L: Match people to places. Write down ticket quantities and prices. S: Buy tickets.	L: Identify the correct pictures. W: Paragraphs. Write a diary entry.
Geography p24 Hurricanes	*(Hurricanes) last (more than a month).* *(A hurricane) caused (a terrible natural disaster).* *(Its name) was (Katrina).*	Project: Make a weather wheel and write about the weather for a week.	
Review 1 p26	Phonics: /ɪd/ /t/ /d/ (*-ed* endings)		
Story Time 1 p28 Robinson Crusoe	*(I) swim (to the ship).* *(I) make (a tent in a cave).* *Is there (a man in the trees)?*		
3 The accident p30	Past simple irregular (affirmative, negative and questions)	R: A letter about last weekend L: Number pictures of places in order. Match people, places and illnesses. S: Make excuses and apologies.	L: Match feelings to situations. W: *on/in/at* with expressions of time Write a letter about last weekend.
Technology p38 Communication	*(Writing) started (7,000 years ago).* *(Many families) had (a telephone).* *(They) didn't have (computers).*	Project: Make a poster about communication technology in your home.	
4 On the train p40	Prepositions of movement: *along, past, across, around, through* Quantifiers: *How much/many? Is there much …?/Are there many …? There isn't much/aren't many …*	R: A description of a school trip L: Identify the foods people order. S: Order food in a restaurant.	L: Match sentences to the correct picture. W: *first, then, afterwards, finally* Write about a school trip.
Geography p48 Map reading	*Walk across (Southwark Bridge).* *Walk past (Waterloo Bridge).* *Go along (Whitehall).*	Project: Make a leaflet about interesting places in your town.	
Review 2 p50	Phonics: /h/ /w/		
Story Time 2 p52 Alice in Wonderland	*There was (a tree in front of the house).* *(Alice) looked (at the watch).* *(He) put (it in his tea).*		
5 Whose bag is it? p54	Possessive *'s* Possessive pronouns: *mine, yours, his, hers, ours, theirs* *have to/don't have to*	R: A description of a daily routine L: Match people to activities. Identify the times activities happen. S: Discuss timetables.	L: Number pictures in order. W: Writing the time. Write about last Saturday.

Unit	Language	Skills: Pupils' Book	Skills: Activity Book
History p62 Clothes through the ages	(Clothes) didn't change (much). (Boys) wore (a short tunic). There were (many different fashions).	Project: Draw and write about your favourite clothes and when you wear them.	
6 The chase p64	Comparative and superlative adjectives with -er and -est (plus some irregulars)	R: An advertisement for a bicycle shop L: Identify the shoes Mel wants to buy. S: Discuss adverts and purchases.	L: Identify the correct pictures. W: Order of adjectives. Write an advertisement.
Science p72 Planets	(The planet) nearest (to the sun is Mercury). (It's) the fastest (planet). (Mars is) smaller than (Earth).	Project: Choose a planet and write about it.	
Review 3 p74	Phonics/Spelling: silent letters		
Story Time 3 p76 The Prince and the Pauper	(Every day Tom) went (to the palace). (He) begged (on the way). (He) ran (out of the room).		
7 They've got Oscar! p78	want to + verb like/enjoy + -ing I'm good at/I'm happy when I'm + -ing. Shall we ...? What about + -ing?	R: An email about weekend plans L: Number holiday posters in order. Identify the activity people want to do. S: Make plans.	L: Identify the correct pictures. W: Using or in questions. Write an email to make plans.
PE p86 Sporting legends	(He's one of) the best (footballers in the world). (He) was good at (football). He's happy when he's (swimming).	Project: Find out and write about a sporting legend from your country.	
8 The rescue p88	going to future (affirmative, negative and questions) Why ...? Because ...	R: An invitation to a party L: Identify occasion, date, time and place. S: Invite someone to a party.	L: Identify if statements about a picture are true or false. W: Writing dates. Write an invitation to a party.
Social Science p96 Duke of Edinburgh's Award	(You) can (help people). (You) camp (for one night). What are you going to do?	Project: Complete a Duke of Edinburgh's Award plan.	
Review 4 p98	Phonics: /ð/ /θ/ /tr/		
Story Time 4 p100 The Voyages of Sindbad the Sailor	I'm going to (make one last voyage). (It) was (a long and dangerous voyage). (I) heard (shouts).		
9 Home again p102	Review: present simple, present continuous, was/were/wasn't/ weren't, past simple regular and irregular, going to future	R: A postcard L: Match people to places. Complete information about what people need to take on a trip. S: Give travel advice.	L: Identify the correct pictures. W: Writing an address. Write a postcard.
Geography p110 The Arctic and Antarctic	(The Arctic and Antarctic are) the coldest (places on Earth). (It's) colder than (the Arctic).	Project: Design and make a poster about your country for a visitor.	
Goodbye! p112	What was your favourite part of the story?		
Review 5 p114	Phonics: /ɪ/ /aɪ/ /ɒ/ /əʊ/ /æ/ /eɪ/		

The Yazoo Show p116

Teacher's Day p118

Valentine's Day p120

The Queen's Birthday p122

Word list p124

Irregular verbs p127

Welcome!

1 Listen and say. Then listen and read. ◀))

detective

missing

① Hello, Jack. Hello, Kelly.

Hello, Aunt Sophie!

Hi, Oscar!

② Who are they?

They're our friends at school.

Mel, Beth, Harry and Kit.

2 Match.

| ① Dr Wild/Aunt Sophie | ② Jack | ③ Kelly | ④ Oscar |

a

b

c

d

3 Sing. •))

Our Aunt Sophie is really cool.
We stay with her when we haven't got school.
She's Dr Wild, Animal Detective!
Dr Wild, Animal Detective!
She can find your animals for you!

Is an animal missing from the zoo?
Ask Dr Wild. She can help you!
She's Dr Wild, Animal Detective!
Dr Wild, Animal Detective!
She can find your animals for you!

4 Read the story again and write True or False.

1 Jack and Kelly are brother and sister. __True__
2 Dr Wild is their aunt. _____
3 Oscar is their friend from school. _____

4 Mel, Harry, Kit and Beth are their friends from school. _____
5 Dr Wild is a teacher. _____
6 Dr Wild can find missing animals. _____

1 Listen and say. Then listen and read. •))

 niece

 nephew

 clever

 lazy

 friendly

 helpful

1 Dr Wild, Animal Detective!

Hello, it's Sally here. I can't find Toto the toucan. He isn't in the zoo! Can you help me?

2 Yes, of course. What does Toto look like?

He's black and white. He's funny and clever. He likes bananas.

3 My niece Kelly and my nephew Jack are with me. And my cat Oscar, of course!

4 Oscar?

Yes, he's lazy but he's very friendly. We can all help.

Thank you. You're very helpful.

5 Does Sally work at the zoo, Aunt Sophie?

Yes, she does.

What does she do?

She's a keeper. She's very kind. She loves animals.

6 Do you know where Toto is?

No, I don't. I don't know where Toto is.

MISSING!
NAME: TOTO
COLOUR: BLACK AND WHITE
HOBBIES: EATING BANANAS

2 Let's learn! Read.

I/You/We/They	He/She/It
I live with Dr Wild.	Dr Wild works at home.
We don't live at the zoo.	She doesn't work at the zoo.
Do Kelly and Jack live with you?	Does she like animals?
No, they don't.	Yes, she does.

3 Read the story again and answer.

1 Does Dr Wild work at the zoo? _No, she doesn't._

2 What does Toto look like? _____

3 Does he like bananas? _____

4 Is Oscar the cat friendly? _____

5 Where does Sally work? _____

6 Does Dr Wild know where Toto is?
_____

4 Listen and tick. •))

	lazy	helpful	kind	funny	clever
(boy and girl)		✔			
(cat)					
(woman)					

5 Look, ask and answer.

Name : **Sophie Wild**
Age : **30**
Hair : **Brown**
Eyes : **Green**
Job : **Animal Detective**
Nationality : **British**
Home Town : **Bristol**
Hobbies : **Flying planes, reading, sport**

1 What's her name?

2 How old is she?

3 What colour is her hair?

4 What colour are her eyes?

5 What's her job?

6 What nationality is she?

7 Where does she live?

8 What are her hobbies?

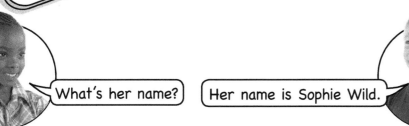

What's her name?

Her name is Sophie Wild.

7

1b We're getting ready!

1 Listen and say. Then listen and read. •))

 laptop

 binoculars

 compass

 can opener

 torch

 diary

 need

Harry: Mel, Beth, Kit, come and see! Jack, Kelly and Dr Wild are talking on the video on my laptop. Hi, Jack! Hi, Kelly! What are you doing?

Jack: Hi, Harry. We're getting ready to find Toto the toucan.

Harry: Are you packing your bags?

Jack: Yes, we are.

Harry: What are you taking?

Jack: I'm taking my binoculars, a compass and a can opener!

Harry: Great!

Jack: We need a torch!

Kelly: I've got one! I'm taking my diary, too.

Dr Wild: I've got my laptop and our passports. That's it. We're ready.

Kelly: Come on, Oscar. We're leaving!

2 Read the story again and write.

1 <u>Jack has got his binoculars.</u>

2 _____

3 _____

4 _____

5 _____

6  _____

7 _____

③ Let's learn! Read.

I/You/We/They

What are you doing?
Are you sleeping, Oscar?
No, I'm not. I'm watching Jack and Kelly.
What are they doing? They're packing their bags.

He/She/It

He's taking a can opener.
She's taking my food.

④ Look, ask and answer.

wearing   eating   drinking   doing homework   talking   reading   listening   writing

Mel   Harry   Beth   Kit

Is Beth eating an apple?

No, she isn't. She's eating a sandwich.

What's she wearing?

She's wearing a pink T-shirt.

⑤ Choose and write.

torch   ~~compass~~   binoculars   diary   can opener   laptop

1 Where am I? Where do I go now?
   I need a ____compass____ .

2 He's reading an email on his _____ .

3 I'm watching birds with my _____ .

4 It's dark. I can't see! I need a _____ .

5 I write in my _____ every day.

6 I can't open this can of fish.
   I need a _____ .

⑥ Listen, choose and write. Then sing. •))

find   ~~looking~~   black   is   know   want   don't   isn't   called

We're (1) ____looking____ for a bird called Toto.
We don't (2) _____ where he is.
He (3) _____ in the zoo,
We (4) _____ know where to go.
We (5) _____ to find him!

We're looking for a bird (6) _____ Toto.
We don't know where he (7) _____ .
He's (8) _____ and white,
We hope he's all right.
We want to (9) _____ him!

Dr Wild drives well.

1 **Listen and say. Then listen and read.** •))

 carefully

 badly

 well

 slowly

 quietly

 happily

 quickly

Dr Wild drives carefully. She doesn't drive badly. She drives well.

Kelly sees a feather in the road!

Dr Wild stops the car slowly.

They look at the feather.

'Toto has got feathers like this,' says Jack quietly. 'I think it's his feather.'

'Yes!' says Kelly happily. She can see two more feathers.

'I need the binoculars, please, Jack,' says Dr Wild.

She can see a man and a woman in a small boat.

'I think that is Claudia Fox and Magnus Wolf. They're very bad people!

We need a boat!' she says. 'Come on! Quickly!'

2 Let's learn! Read.

Dr Wild drives carefully.   careful   carefully
Oscar sleeps quietly.   quiet   quietly
                           happy   happily
                           good   well

3 Read the story again and write True or False.

1 Dr Wild drives carefully and well. __True__
2 She stops the car quickly. _____
3 They can see black feathers. _____

4 Kelly can see Toto. _____
5 Dr Wild likes Claudia and Magnus. _____

4 Look, match and write.

~~badly~~ happily well quickly slowly quietly

1 __f__ He's drawing __badly__ .
2 _____ She's singing _____ .
3 _____ They're walking _____ .

4 _____ She's running _____ .
5 _____ They're playing _____ .
6 _____ He's sleeping _____ .

5 Think and write with Dr Wild.

drive talk eat run sing draw write read

Think about you, your friends and your family. How do they do these things?

My friend Pauline talks quickly.
_____
_____
_____
_____
_____
_____

1 **Look at the photo and say. What can we learn about Mel?**

She reads books.

All about me

My name is Mel Taylor. I live in Bristol in England. I'm tall and I've got
(1) short / long (2) brown / red hair and
(3) brown / green eyes. I've got a small family, my mum, my dad, my
(4) sister / brother and me. I love my phone. It's pink and I use it every day to talk to my friends. I'm friendly and I think I'm helpful, too. At the weekends I always help my mum and dad in the house and then go out with my friends. I sometimes play on the computer,
I (5) read / draw and
(6) play volleyball / go swimming.
(7) Volleyball / Swimming is my favourite sport — I swim
(8) slowly / quickly and (9) well / badly.

2 **Look, read and circle in 1.**

3 **Read again and answer.**

1 Where does Mel live?

_____In Bristol._____

2 What are her hobbies?

_____

3 What does she do at the weekends?

_____

4 Is she lazy?

_____

4. Listen and write the numbers. Then ask your friends and write. •))

name	Mel
number	6754430

name	Beth
number	

name	Harry
number	

name	Kit
number	

What's your phone number?

It's ...

name	
number	

name	
number	

name	
number	

name	
number	

5. Listen and circle. •))

1 Where's Kit?

2 What's he doing?

3 What does he want to do later?

4 Where's Mel?

5 What's she doing?

6 What does she want to do later?

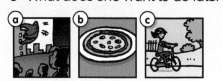

6. Choose places and activities from 5 and write. Then act it out.

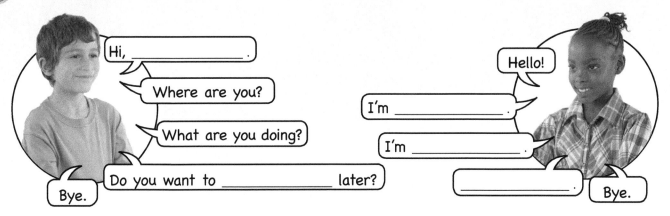

Hi, _____ .

Where are you?

What are you doing?

Do you want to _____ later?

Bye.

Hello!

I'm _____ .

I'm _____ .

_____ . Bye.

13

Music

1 **Listen and guess. Say where the music is from.** •))

It's from Australia.

Australian didgeridoo music

2 **Listen and match the countries to the pictures.** •))

3 **Read and label the photos in 1.**

Scottish bagpipe music
Bagpipes are very old instruments. You **blow** them and they make a **loud** noise. You don't dance to the music of the bagpipes but you can walk quickly to it.

Argentinian tango music
The **tango** is a popular dance in Argentina. Sometimes you dance the tango quickly, and sometimes you move slowly and carefully.

Chinese opera music
In Chinese **operas** the actors paint their faces with different colours. They sing and wear masks and hats. Sometimes there's a very exciting lion dance. You can hear drums and **bells** in this music.

Polish polonaise music
The **polonaise** is a dance. In Poland girls and boys dance the polonaise together at school parties. They move slowly and beautifully. You can play polonaise music by the **composer** Chopin on the piano.

Australian didgeridoo music
The **didgeridoo** is an old instrument. It's long and you blow it. It's loud and it's difficult to play well. You don't dance or sing to didgeridoo music.

4 **Read again and write True or False.**

1 You dance to the bagpipes. ___False___
2 You always dance the tango quickly. _____
3 There are drums in Chinese opera music. _____

4 The polonaise is a fast, exciting dance. _____
5 It's easy to play the didgeridoo. _____

5 **Your project!** Make a leaflet about music in your country.

Come to Turkey and listen to the amazing baglama! The baglama is an old instrument. You can dance and sing to the baglama. Sometimes the music is fast and sometimes it's slow. It's always beautiful!

2a There was a storm.

1 **Listen and say. Then listen and read.** •))

storm

thunder and lightning

worried

windy

behind

in front of

Yesterday evening we were on a small boat. Claudia and Magnus were on a boat, too. We were behind their boat. We were near Toto but Dr Wild was worried. There were big black clouds in the sky. Suddenly there was lots of rain and it was very windy. There was a terrible storm with thunder and lightning. It was a bad night on the boat.

In the morning it was sunny and we were safe but there weren't any boats near us. Claudia and Magnus weren't in front of us. We were near a beach and there was a town not far away. But where were Claudia and Magnus? Where was Toto? Were they in the town?

2 Let's learn! Read.

There was a storm.
Was there a town?
There were black clouds.
Were there any people?

There wasn't a boat in front of them.
Yes, there was. / No, there wasn't.
There weren't any boats behind them.
Yes, there were. / No, there weren't.

3 Read the story again and write True or False.

1 Dr Wild was on a big boat. ___False___

2 Jack was worried. _____

3 It was windy and there was a storm in the night. _____

4 There was thunder and lightning in the morning. _____

5 There weren't any boats behind them in the morning. _____

6 There was a town near the beach. _____

4 Listen and number. Then ask and answer. •))

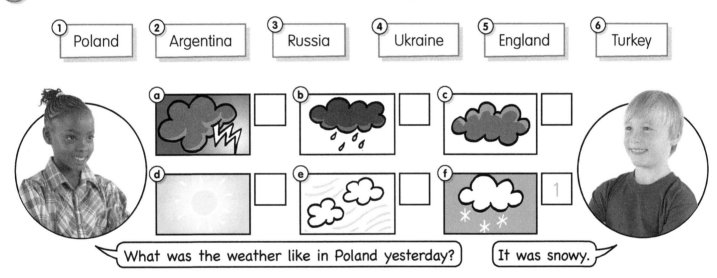

① Poland ② Argentina ③ Russia ④ Ukraine ⑤ England ⑥ Turkey

What was the weather like in Poland yesterday?

It was snowy.

5 Look and say. Use There was/were or There wasn't/weren't.

two big boats in the sea

any sand on the beach

two children with their mum

one small boat

any clouds in the sky

There wasn't any sand on the beach.

We were here last summer.

2b We landed on a beach.

1 Listen and say. Then listen and read. •))

aquarium

town hall

police station

pet shop

museum

café

follow

We've got an email from Jack and Kelly.

Can you read it, Harry?

To: Harry@yazoo.com, Beth@yazoo.com
From: Jack@yazoo.com
Subject: We landed on a beach!

Hello,

How are you? We're having an exciting trip.

Yesterday we landed on a beach in France. Then we walked to a town. It wasn't far. We looked for Toto all morning. He wasn't in the park. He wasn't in the zoo but Oscar liked the aquarium. We asked about Toto in the town hall and the police station. We looked in the pet shop. There were some pretty yellow birds and a funny parrot but Toto wasn't there. In the afternoon we visited the library and the museum. In the museum we followed a short man and a tall woman to a café but it wasn't Claudia and Magnus! The café makes very good cakes!

We're very worried. We can't find Toto.

Email us soon.

Kelly and Jack

2 Read the story again and match.

1 Jack and Kelly are in   a a zoo.
2 There was an aquarium and   b the café.
3 There were some yellow birds in   c Toto.
4 There were some very good cakes in d the pet shop.
5 Jack and Kelly can't find   e a town in France.

3 Let's learn! Read.

Yesterday we landed on a beach.   We walked to a town.
We looked for Toto.

4 Listen and circle. Then say. •))

1 ask for help
/ a map

2 look at the dinosaurs
/ the watches

3 wait for a friend
/ a table

Yesterday Magnus
asked for a map.

4 watch the fish
/ the sharks

5 play with a rabbit
/ a dog

6 listen to a talk about birds
/ a concert

5 Look at 4 and write.

1 He ___asked for a map___ in the
police station.

2 They _____ in the museum.

3 She _____ in the café.

4 They _____ in
the aquarium.

5 She _____ in the pet shop.

6 They _____ in the
town hall.

6 Listen and number the pictures. Then sing. •))

1

① Yesterday I stayed at home.
Yesterday I helped my dad.
Yesterday I washed the car,
Yesterday morning.

② Yesterday I walked to the park.
Yesterday I played with my friends.
Yesterday I jumped and skipped,
Yesterday afternoon.

③ Yesterday I watched TV.
Yesterday I listened to music.
Yesterday I looked at the stars,
Yesterday evening.

1 Listen and say. Then listen and read. 🔊

moustache

beard

face

blond

thin

wavy

notice

1 Kelly and Jack didn't find Toto yesterday. They decided to ask for help.

Excuse me. We're looking for this bird. Can you help us?

Yes, I can.

2 This morning a car stopped here. There was a toucan in the car.

3 Did you notice a man and a woman in the car?

Yes, I did.

What did the man look like?

4 He was short with a blond moustache and beard.

5 And the woman?

The woman was tall and thin with wavy hair. I didn't look at her face.

It was Magnus and Claudia.

6 Did you talk to them?

No, I didn't. Look! That's the car.

Quick! Follow them.

Thank you.

20

2 Let's learn! Read.

Did you notice a man and a woman?   Yes, I did.
Did they look at you?   No, they didn't.
What did they look like?   I don't know. I didn't look carefully.

3 Read the story again and circle.

1 Kelly showed / didn't show the boy a photo of Toto.

2 A car stopped / didn't stop near the boy in the morning.

3 The boy noticed / didn't notice a toucan in the car.

4 The boy looked / didn't look at Magnus and Claudia.

5 The boy talked / didn't talk to Magnus and Claudia.

6 The boy followed / didn't follow Magnus and Claudia.

4 Read and match. Then ask and answer.

 a    b    c    d

Picture a: What did he look like?

1 He was tall with a black moustache and beard. __b__

2 She was thin with wavy brown hair and glasses. _____

3 He was not very tall with short blond hair and blue eyes. _____

4 She was pretty with long red hair and brown eyes. _____

5 Think and write with Dr Wild.

Look: short/tall/thin/pretty   **Hair:** long/short/wavy + colour
Eyes: blue/brown/green/grey   **Other:** beard/moustache/glasses

Think of a man or woman you remember from a film or book. What did he or she look like?

The man was tall with short brown hair, blue eyes and a moustache.

I'd like tickets for the museum, please.

2d
SKILLS

1 Look at the photos and guess what Harry did.

> Picture 1: He looked at some old computers.

November

17 Saturday

It was cold and windy today. In the morning I walked to the park with Beth. We played on the swings and the slide in the playground. I climbed a tree and Beth watched me.

After lunch we visited the Science Museum and looked at the old computers. There was a café behind the museum. Beth wanted a strawberry ice cream but I wanted a chocolate cake. The cake was very good.

There was a storm in the evening and it was horrible outside. I stayed at home and watched a film with my mum. It was about a spy with a funny moustache and beard. I liked the film but my mum didn't like it.

① _____

② _____

③ _____ morning _____

2 Read and label the photos morning, afternoon or evening.

3 Read again and answer.

1 Did Harry walk to the park with Mel?
No, he walked to the park with Beth.

2 Did Beth climb the tree?
_____

3 Did Harry and Beth look at old computers in the museum?
_____

4 Did Beth want a strawberry ice cream?
_____

5 Did Harry and his mum go to the cinema?
_____

6 Did Harry watch a spy film with his mum?
_____

22 ✎ Writing class: AB, page 20

4 Listen and number. Then say. •))

a	b	c	d
			1

Beth   Kit   Mel   Harry

Number 1.

Yes, I'd like tickets for the museum, please.

Can I help you?

5 Listen again and write. •))

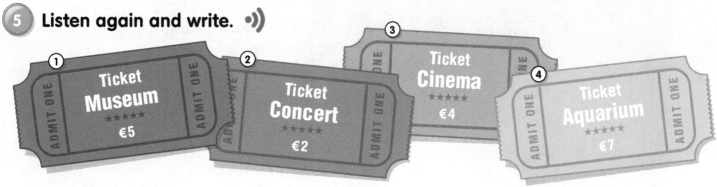

① Ticket **Museum** ★★★★★ €5

② Ticket **Concert** ★★★★★ €2

③ Ticket **Cinema** ★★★★★ €4

④ Ticket **Aquarium** ★★★★★ €7

1 Tickets __2__   Euros __10__
2 Tickets _____   Euros _____

3 Tickets _____   Euros _____
4 Tickets _____   Euros _____

6 Choose a place from 5 and write. Then act it out.

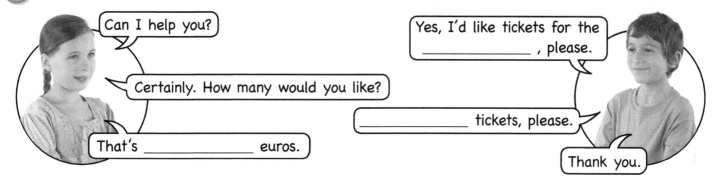

Can I help you?

Yes, I'd like tickets for the _____ , please.

Certainly. How many would you like?

_____ tickets, please.

That's _____ euros.

Thank you.

Geography

1 **Look and guess. Tick the true sentences.**

This is a **hurricane.**

a Hurricanes **last** more than a month. _____

b Hurricanes can be 1,000 kilometres across. ✔

2 This is a **flood.**

a Hurricanes **cause** floods. _____

b There aren't any floods in towns. _____

This is a **tornado.**

a Hurricanes can **produce** tornadoes. _____

b The winds **travel** at 3,000 kilometres an hour. _____

4 Winds and floods **destroy** houses.

a A hurricane destroyed the capital city of England. _____

b A hurricane caused a terrible **natural disaster** in the USA. _____

2 Read and check.

A hurricane is a very big storm with lots of rain and strong winds. Hurricanes can be 1,000 kilometres across. They last for more than a week. The winds are 120 to 300 kilometres an hour. Sometimes the hurricane winds produce tornadoes.

Hurricanes come between May and November when the ocean is warm. A hurricane starts over the ocean and moves from east to west. It moves about 25 kilometres every hour. When it comes on land, it causes floods and people must move to a different town. Some years there are lots of hurricanes and some years there aren't many.

Every hurricane has a name. In August 2005 there was a very strong hurricane in the USA. Its name was Katrina. The winds destroyed many houses, trees and cars and there were bad floods, especially in the beautiful old city of New Orleans. It was a very bad natural disaster and many people died.

3 Read again and write True or False.

1 A hurricane is a very big snow storm. ___False___

2 Hurricanes come between November and May. _____

3 Hurricanes move about 25 kilometres every hour. _____

4 There are lots of hurricanes every year. _____

5 Every hurricane has a name. _____

6 There was a terrible natural disaster in America in 2005. _____

4 **Your project!** Make a weather wheel and write about the weather for a week.

On Monday it was cold and windy.
On Tuesday it rained in the morning.
In the afternoon it was cloudy.
On Wednesday it was cloudy and the
sky was grey all day.
On Thursday there was a storm with
thunder and lightning.
On Friday it was sunny and hot and
there wasn't any wind.

My Weather Wheel

Today's Weather is:

Peter

Review 1

1 Read and circle.

Harry: Who (1) did / do you stay with last weekend, Beth?

Beth: My sister and I (2) stayed / staying with my grandma and grandpa. It was great! On Saturday we (3) walked / played to the pet shop but it wasn't open so we (4) listened / visited the aquarium instead.

Harry: Did you (5) like / liked the aquarium?

Beth: I loved the sharks. They (6) was / were amazing.

Harry: What about Sunday?

Beth: On Sunday we (7) visited / decided the museum. The dinosaurs (8) was / were my favourite but my sister (9) did / didn't like them and she cried. She's so funny!

2 Listen and tick the correct pictures. •))

1 ⓐ  ✓   ⓑ  ☐

2 ⓐ  ☐   ⓑ  ☐

3 ⓐ  ☐   ⓑ ☐

3 What about you? Choose and write.

dance ~~speak English~~ drive sing write talk swim walk
~~well~~ badly slowly quietly quickly carefully happily

1 My teacher _speaks English well_ .

2 I _____ .

3 My dad _____ .

4 My friend _____ .

5 My mum _____ .

6 _____

4 Listen and chant. •))

I visited the zoo, watched a kangaroo.
He played with me, too!

26

Play the game.

What's the weather like?

It's stormy.

Where's the boy?

He's in front of the library.

What has he got?

He's got an umbrella.

It's number 12.

That's right!

Robinson Crusoe

1 **Read and listen.** 🔊

PENGUIN READERS

Robinson Crusoe

Daniel Defoe

In September 1659 I leave Brazil for Africa with ten other men. It's very hot and the weather is good. But after 12 days there's a great storm. The sea plays with me for a very long time. It leaves me on the beach. I'm very tired and I'm not well. Where are all the other men? I don't know.

The sea is quiet now. I've got nothing with me – no food, no **tools** and no **knife**. I swim to the ship and find many important things there: food and drink, pens and paper, money, clothes, knives, books. I make a small boat and make 11 **journey**s between the beach and the ship. Then the storms start again and I stay on **land**.

The wind and rain are strong all night. The next morning I can't see the ship. It's under the sea, with my ten friends.

I'm on an **island**. I find a place for my home. I make a tent in a **cave**. I cut down young trees and build a strong wall around my home. I have two rooms in my home. I live and sleep in the tent and I use the cave for my food and water.

There's rain every day for two months from the middle of August to the middle of October. I can't leave my house because of the rain but I'm busy.

The end of September is a sad day for me. One year on this island. One year with no people and no talking. I'm very quiet and sad all day.

Then one day I go to the beach and I see something **strange**. It's a man's **footprint**. How is this possible? I walk up and down the beach and look at the mark again. Strange ideas are in my head. Is there a man in the trees? Who's on my island?

I stay in my house for three days. I can't sleep. Are there other people on the island?

② Find and write.

①

_____cave_____
a space inside a mountain

②

_____
you make this when you walk on the beach

③

_____
this is land with sea all around it

④

_____
going from one place to another

⑤

_____
you use this to cut things

⑥

_____
we live on this, fish live in the sea

⑦

_____
not like things you know or see every day

⑧

_____
you use these to make things

Magnus and Claudia had an accident!

1 Listen and say. Then listen and read.

 farm
 cow
 grass
 owl
 pond
 bull

1 Where are Magnus and Claudia?
I saw their car. But where is it now?

2 They went to that farm, I think! I can see a horse and some cows eating grass.

Magnus and Claudia had an accident!

3 It was an owl.
What was that noise?
No. I heard a crash!

4 Magnus drove into a tree!

5 They fell in the duck pond! They're wet and angry!
The ducks are angry, too!

6 The cow is angry, too!
That's not a cow. It's a bull!

2 Let's learn! Read.

see	saw	have	had
go	went	drive	drove
hear	heard	fall	fell

Magnus drives badly. Yesterday he drove into a tree!

3 Read the story again and correct one word.

1 Claudia and Magnus went to a shop. __farm__   4 They were wet and happy. _____

2 Magnus walked into a tree. _____   5 There were cows, ducks, an owl, a horse and

3 They swam in a duck pond. _____   a mouse on the farm. _____

4 Listen and number. •))

5 Choose and write in the past form. Then say.

~~have~~ see go hear drive fall

1 ____had____ a bad day

2 _____ to a farm

3 _____ badly

4 _____ in a duck pond

5 _____ strange noises

6 _____ a bull

Claudia and Magnus had a bad day yesterday.

31

3b Did they find Toto?

1 Listen and say. Then listen and read. •))

 scared

 confused

 nervous

 unhappy

We got some photos and an email from Kelly and Jack.

Did they find Toto?

No, they didn't!

To: Harry@yazoo.com, Beth@yazoo.com, Mel@yazoo.com

From: Kelly@yazoo.com

Subject: Claudia and Magnus had an accident!

Hi all!

We saw Claudia and Magnus yesterday. They crashed their car! We didn't speak to them and we didn't find Toto. Aunt Sophie is worried. Oscar didn't like the farm and he didn't sleep well. The cows were very big and he was scared. He didn't know what the owls were. He thought they were flying cats. He was confused! The bull was very big and noisy and Oscar was nervous all night. He didn't want the bull to chase him. Poor Oscar, he was very unhappy! We took some photos of Claudia and Magnus yesterday. Here they are!

Hope you are all OK.

Love Kelly and Jack

2 Choose and write.

They didn't like this animal!   ~~Magnus drove very badly!~~   They didn't see the pond!

Beth: Did Claudia and Magnus have an accident?

Harry: Yes, they did. _Magnus drove very badly!_

Mel: Did they fall in?

Harry: Yes, they did. _____

_____

_____

Beth: Did the bull chase them?

Harry: Yes, it did. _____

_____

_____

32

3 Let's learn! Read.

Did Oscar sleep well?   Did he hear the owl?
No, he didn't. He didn't sleep all night.   Yes, he did.

4 Choose and write.

~~nervous~~   unhappy   scared   confused

Look at all those people!   Help! I don't like big dogs.   Where do I go? Here or there?   My friend isn't talking to me today.

1 _She's nervous._   **2** _____   **3** _____   **4** _____

5 Choose and write. Then write four questions, ask and answer.

~~go~~   see   have

1 _____go_____ out with your friends/to the cinema/to school
2 _____ bread and honey for breakfast/a good time at school/fun
3 _____ a white cat/your best friend/a funny film

1 _Did you go out with your friends yesterday?_   **3** _____
2 _____   **4** _____

(Did you go out with your friends yesterday?) (No, I didn't.)

6 Listen, choose and write. Then sing.

Did   Was   see   hear   ~~have~~   laugh   dance

Did you (1) _have_ a good day yesterday?

Did you sing? Did you (2) _____ ?
Did you play?

(3) _____ you talk to your friends

And (4) _____ with them, too?

Did you look at the sky?

(5) _____ it grey, was it blue?

Did you (6) _____ the wind blowing?

Did you go to the sea?

Did you (7) _____ the birds flying

And sitting in trees?

Did you have a good day yesterday?

Did you have a good day yesterday?

1 Listen and say. Then listen and read.

cold   headache   sore throat   earache   stomachache   well   ill

Claudia and Magnus went to a small hotel with Toto. They were ill after they fell in the duck pond. They had colds. They didn't go out; they stayed in their rooms. Magnus had a sore throat and a headache. He was hungry and unhappy. Claudia made a big sandwich but Magnus didn't eat it. He ate ice cream and he drank hot tea. He didn't read; he watched TV. Claudia had earache and stomachache. She didn't eat ice cream, she didn't drink tea and she didn't watch TV. She drank water, read a book and wrote her diary. Toto sat in his cage. He was very unhappy, too. He didn't like Claudia or Magnus.

Let's learn! Read.

read	read	drink	drank
make	made	write	wrote
eat	ate	sit	sat

I didn't eat ice cream. I ate a fish!

3 **Read the story again and tick the true sentences.**

1 **a** Claudia and Magnus were ill __✔__
   b Claudia and Magnus were well_____

2 **a** Claudia had a headache and Magnus had earache. _____
   b Magnus had a headache and Claudia had earache. _____

3 **a** Claudia made ice cream. _____
   b Claudia made a sandwich. _____

4 **a** Magnus ate, drank and watched TV. _____
   b Magnus ate, drank and read a book. _____

4 **Look, choose and write.**

headache ~~earache~~ stomachache sore throat cold

① _____earache_____

② _____

③ _____

④ _____

⑤ _____

5 **Think and write with Dr Wild.**

drink   make   eat   write   go   see   read

Write what you did and didn't do yesterday.

I drank some orange juice for breakfast.
I didn't make my bed.
_____
_____
_____

3d
SKILLS

I'm sorry I didn't come.

1 **Look at the pictures of Mel and say.**

In picture 1a Mel isn't with her grandma and grandpa. In picture 1b Mel is with them.

Bristol
March 20th

Dear Grandma,

How are you? I hope you are well.

I'm sorry I didn't come to your birthday dinner on Sunday. I was ill.

I went to a farm with my friend Beth on Saturday. We arrived at ten o'clock in the morning. It was sunny then and I didn't wear my coat but in the afternoon it rained. There were lots of cows on the farm. Beth didn't like them. She was scared. I thought that was funny! Cows aren't scary! There was a horse there, too. Beth can ride horses but I can't. I fell off lots of times. She thought that was funny!

The next day I had a cold and a sore throat. I didn't go to school on Monday but I'm well again now.

I hope you had a nice time on your birthday. Seventy years old. That's great!

Give my love to Grandpa.

Love from Mel

1

2

3

2 **Read and answer.**

1 Who is the letter to and how does it start? <u>It's to Grandma. It starts 'Dear Grandma'.</u>

2 Who is the letter from and how does it finish? _____

3 Where did Mel and Beth go on Saturday? _____

3 **Read again and tick the correct pictures.**

4 Listen and number. •))

5 Listen again and match. Then say. •))

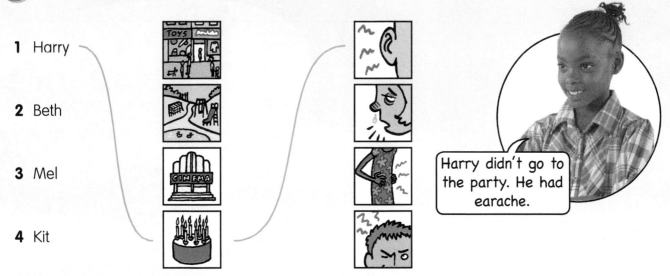

1 Harry

2 Beth

3 Mel

4 Kit

Harry didn't go to the party. He had earache.

6 Choose places and illnesses from 5 and write. Then act it out.

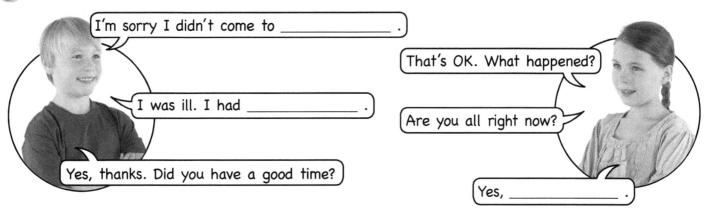

I'm sorry I didn't come to _____ .

That's OK. What happened?

I was ill. I had _____ .

Are you all right now?

Yes, thanks. Did you have a good time?

Yes, _____ .

Technology

1 Look and answer.

How are these people communicating?

Picture 1: She's listening to the radio.

2 Match. Then tick.

	Type of communication		
	talking/listening	reading/writing	using a machine
a mobile phone _6_	✓		✓
b newspaper _____			
c e-book reader _____			
d TV _____			
e computer _____			
f radio _____			
g letter _____			

3 Read and complete the timeline.

books   radio and TV   ~~writing~~   computers   newspapers

Today we **communicate** in lots of different ways. But thousands of years ago there were no books, no phones, no radios, no TVs, no computers and people didn't write.

Writing started about 5,000 years ago. The Egyptians wrote with pictures called 'hieroglyphs'. There weren't any books and there wasn't any **paper**. People wrote on **clay**, wood or leaves. The Chinese made the first paper 2,000 years ago. After that books **appeared**. People in Europe made the first newspapers about 550 years ago.

50 years ago, when your grandparents were young, people listened to the radio and watched TV but they didn't have computers. The first computers were very, very big. They were the **size** of a room! Many families had a telephone at home but there weren't any mobile phones. People didn't use home computers or mobile phones until the 1970s. The first mobile phone was very big and it **weighed** two kilos! Mobile phones today are very small.

Today we have books, phones, radios, TVs and computers. We use these **machines** every day and they're very helpful.

| Old | 1 _writing_ > | 2 _____ > | 3 _____ > | 4 _____ > | 5 _____ > | New |

4 Read again and correct one word.

1 Writing started about 5,000 ~~months~~ ago.
   _____years_____

2 The Chinese made the first computers 2,000 years ago. _____

3 People in Egypt made the first newspapers.
   _____

4 50 years ago lots of people had computers and TVs at home. _____

5 The first mobile phone was small.
   _____

5 Your project! Make a poster about communication in your home.

COMMUNICATION IN MY HOME

I've got some books in my bedroom.

My dad buys a newspaper on Sundays.

There's a radio in the kitchen and a TV in the living room.

My mum and dad have got mobile phones. They always take their mobiles with them.

1 Listen and say. Then listen and read. •))

train station   road   market   castle   bridge   hotel

THIEF STEALS SUITCASE

Jack: Where did Claudia and Magnus go?

Dr Wild: I don't know. They didn't stay at the farm.

Kelly: There's a photo of Magnus in this newspaper. He was at the train station yesterday. I think he bought tickets.

Dr Wild: Yes, that's Magnus. We must go to the station. Have you got the map, Jack?

Jack: Yes, I have. We walk along this road. It goes past the market and around the castle. Then we go across the bridge.

Kelly: Do we go through the park?

Jack: Yes, we do. The station is next to the park.

Dr Wild and the children left the hotel and walked quickly to the station.

Jack: I can see Claudia and Magnus. They're getting on the train. Run!

Dr Wild and the children got on the train with Oscar and it left the station.

2 Let's learn! Read.

Oscar went along the road, past the market, across the bridge, around the castle and through the park.

3 Read the story again and match.

1 Dr Wild and the children went past
2 They went around
3 They went across
4 They went through
5 They went to

a the park.
b the bridge.
c the train station.
d the castle.
e the market.

4 Listen and tick. •))

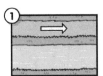 river _____
 road ✔

 castle _____
 train station _____

 supermarket _____
 hotel _____

 bridge _____
 field _____

 market _____
 park _____

5 Draw the route from the house to the beach. Then say.

across   through   around   ~~past~~   along
field   ~~farm~~   forest   beach   mountain

I walked past the farm.

How much were the tickets?

4b

1 Listen and say. Then listen and read. •))

carriage

seat

money

luggage

search

look after

It's Jack on the phone!

Mel: Where are you?

Jack: We're on a train.

Mel: Lucky you. I love trains. How many carriages are there?

Jack: There are five. There are lots of people on the train.

Mel: How many seats are there in each carriage?

Jack: I don't know! Wait … one, two … there are 36!

Mel: How much were the tickets?

Jack: Lots of money – 50 euros!

Mel: Are Claudia and Magnus on the train?

Jack: We think so. Kelly and I are searching every carriage but we can't see any people who look like them. We hope they've got Toto with them.

Mel: What's Dr Wild doing?

Jack: She's looking after the luggage and Oscar.

Mel: How much luggage have you got?

Jack: There's lots of luggage!

Mel: Give our love to Oscar!

Jack: OK!

2 Read the story again and match.

1 Where are Kelly and Jack?
2 Are there lots of people on the train?
3 What are Kelly and Jack doing?
4 Are Claudia and Magnus on the train?
5 What's Dr Wild doing?
6 What does Mel love?

a She's looking after Oscar.
b She loves trains.
c Yes, there are.
d Kelly and Jack think so.
e They're on a train.
f They're searching every carriage.

3 Let's learn! Read.

How much luggage is there?
How much was the ticket?
How many people are there?

There's lots of luggage.
It was 20 euros.
There are three people.

4 Write How much/How many and circle. Then ask and answer.

How much spaghetti is there?

How many apples are there?

There's lots of spaghetti.

There aren't any apples.

1 __How much__ spaghetti (is)/ are there?
2 _____ apples is / are there?
3 _____ tomatoes is / are there?
4 _____ milk is / are there?

5 _____ carrots is / are there?
6 _____ bread is / are there?
7 _____ seats is / are there?
8 _____ money is / are there?

5 Listen and circle. Then sing. •))

We're travelling on the train,
We're travelling on the train.
How (1) (many) / much people can you see
On the train, on the train?
How (2) many / much luggage can you see
On the train, on the train?
There (3) is / are three people, one, two, three
On the train, on the train.
There (4) is / are lots of luggage next to me
On the train, on the train.
We're travelling on the train!

1 Listen and say. Then listen and read. ◀))

stew

rice

cabbage

steak

peas

① Shh! Hide! I can see them. Magnus is eating stew with rice ... and cabbage.

Be careful they don't see you.

② What's Claudia eating?

Steak, peas and chips.

Are there many chips?

Yes, there are lots!

Please can I have some of your peas, Claudia?

③ And is there much rice?

There's lots of rice but there isn't much cabbage.

Listen. I heard a noise. Did you hear it?

⑤ Yes, children and a cat!

④ No! There aren't many peas. I want all my peas!

⑥ I want that cat!

Oscar! Come back!

2 Let's learn! Read.

Is there much rice?
No, there isn't much rice.
Are there many peas?
No, there aren't many peas.

3 Read the story again and write True or False.

1 Jack didn't see Claudia and Magnus. __False__
2 Magnus ate steak and chips. _____
3 Magnus didn't have much cabbage. _____

4 Claudia didn't have many chips. _____
5 Jack and Kelly didn't make much noise. _____
6 Claudia wanted Oscar. _____

4 Look and match. Then ask and answer.

1 chips 2 salad 3 rice 4 stew 5 oranges 6 steaks 7 peas 8 potatoes

Is there much rice?

Are there many oranges?

No, there isn't much rice.

Yes, there are lots of oranges.

5 Think and write with Dr Wild.

chairs blackboards tables food pictures soup milk apples books

Write about the things in your school canteen.

There aren't many pictures in our school canteen. There's lots of soup.

_____

_____

_____

_____

_____

4d

SKILLS

I'd like chips.

1 Look, choose and say.

train station   fish and chips   castle   park   pencil

> In picture a I can see fish and chips.

Our school trip to Windsor Castle

Yesterday our class went on a school trip to Windsor Castle. First we went to the train station and bought our tickets. Then we got on the train. There weren't many people in our carriage. I sat next to Mel. I like trains. We arrived in Windsor at 11 o'clock and we walked across the road to the castle. It's very old. A man showed us around the castle. He told us many stories about the old kings and queens.

Then we had lunch. I had fish. It came with lots of chips but there weren't many peas. Afterwards we walked in Windsor Great Park. Finally we went to the shop and I bought a pencil. It was a wonderful day.

2 Read and number the pictures in order.

3 Read again and answer.

1 Where did the class go yesterday?
   Windsor Castle

2 Were there many people in the carriage?
_____

3 What time did the class arrive in Windsor?
_____

4 What did Beth eat for lunch?
_____

5 What did the class do after lunch?
_____

6 What did Beth buy?
_____

Writing class: AB, page 44

4 Choose and write to complete the menu.

rice   peas   cabbage   steak   milk   ice cream   chips   water   chocolate cake   pizza

1. [H] stew
2. [ ] _____
3. [ ] _____
4. [ ] _____
5. [ ] _____
6. [ ] bread
7. [ ] _____
8. [ ] salad
9. [ ] _____
10. [ ] _____
11. [ ] orange juice
12. [ ] _____
13. [ ] _____
14. [ ] _____
15. [ ] strawberries

QUEEN'S CAFÉ MENU

5 Listen and write H (Harry), K (Kit) or M (Mel). •))

6 Choose foods from 4 and write. Then act it out.

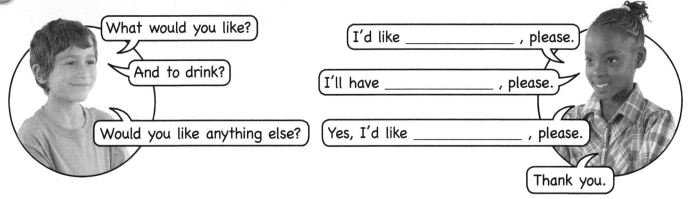

What would you like?

I'd like _____ , please.

And to drink?

I'll have _____ , please.

Would you like anything else?

Yes, I'd like _____ , please.

Thank you.

47

Geography

1 **Read about the famous places in London.**

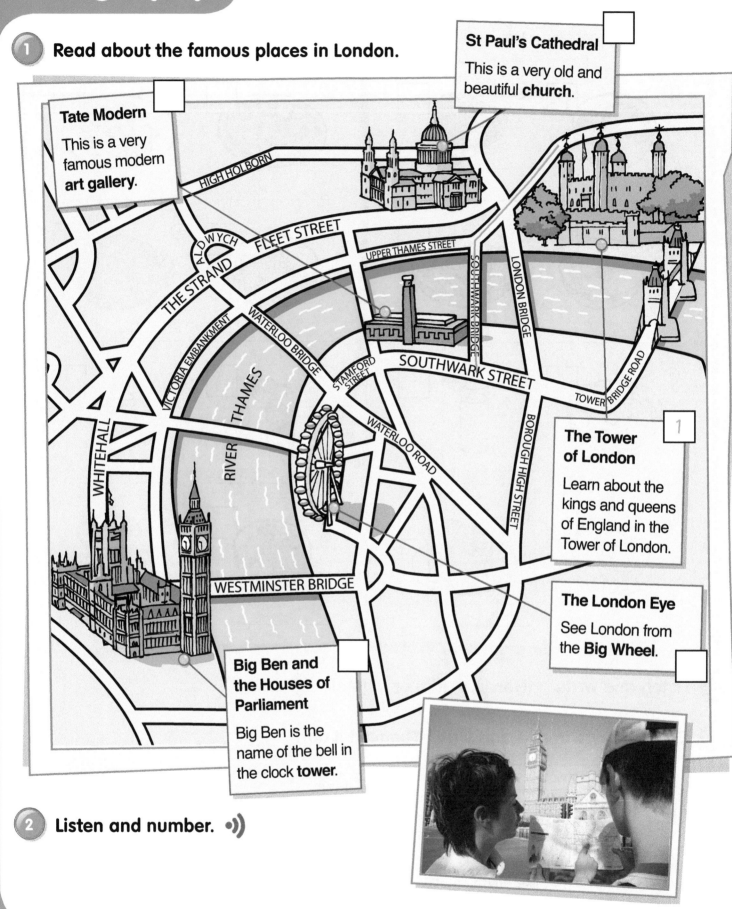

St Paul's Cathedral

This is a very old and beautiful **church**.

Tate Modern

This is a very famous modern **art gallery**.

The Tower of London

Learn about the kings and queens of England in the Tower of London.

1

The London Eye

See London from the **Big Wheel**.

Big Ben and the Houses of Parliament

Big Ben is the name of the bell in the clock **tower**.

HIGH HOLBORN

ALDWYCH

FLEET STREET

THE STRAND

UPPER THAMES STREET

SOUTHWARK BRIDGE

LONDON BRIDGE

VICTORIA EMBANKMENT

WATERLOO BRIDGE

STAMFORD STREET

SOUTHWARK STREET

TOWER BRIDGE ROAD

WHITEHALL

RIVER THAMES

WATERLOO ROAD

BOROUGH HIGH STREET

WESTMINSTER BRIDGE

2 **Listen and number.** •))

48

3 Read and draw the route on the map in 1.

A walking tour of central London

The River Thames goes through London and there are lots of interesting places to visit near the river.

Start at the Tower of London. It's an old **palace** and many kings and queens stayed here. You can see many beautiful **crowns** there.

Walk across Southwark Bridge to the other side of the river to visit Tate Modern. You can see interesting art here and also watch films or visit the restaurant.

Next walk past Waterloo Bridge and go for a ride on the London Eye! It looks like a big bicycle wheel.

Go across Westminster Bridge and see Big Ben. That is the name of the bell in the tower next to the Houses of Parliament. There are four clocks on the tower and you can hear Big Ben every hour.

Finally go along Whitehall, the Strand and Fleet Street to St Paul's **Cathedral**. In 1666 there was a big fire in London and the fire destroyed the old cathedral.

4 Read again and write True or False.

1 Kings and queens live in the Tower of London now. ___False___

2 You can see paintings and films in the Tate Modern. _____

3 You can ride on the London Eye. _____

4 Big Ben is the name of a clock. _____

5 St Paul's Cathedral is on Westminster Bridge. _____

5 Your project! **Make a leaflet about interesting places in your town.**

COME TO BRIDGETOWN!

Come and see the old castle. It's in Main Street.

HERITAGE CENTRE

In High Street there's a History Museum. There are lots of interesting things to see there. There's a famous bridge over the river.

Review 2

1 **Look, choose and write.**

steaks ~~chips~~ peas ~~cabbage~~ rice stew

①  ② ③ ④  ⑤  ⑥

1 How _many chips are there_ ? _There aren't many chips._

2 How _much cabbage is there_ ? _There isn't_

3 How _____ ? _____

4 How _____ ? _____

5 How _____ ? _____

6 How _____ ? _____

2 **Listen and match. Then write and say.** •))

stomachache ~~earache~~ headache cold and sore throat

1 mum ⓐ 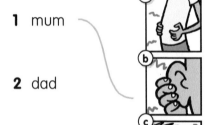 _____ /not eat anything

2 dad ⓑ _____earache_____ /not go to work

3 brother ⓒ _____ /not go to school

4 sister ⓓ _____ /not speak

Her mum had earache.
She didn't go to work.

3 **Listen and chant.** •))

Who's on the horse on the hill?
What's he watching in the water?

50

Alice in Wonderland

1 **Read and listen.** •))

PENGUIN READERS

Alice in Wonderland

Lewis Carroll

The Mad Hatter's Tea Party

There was a tree in front of the house. Under the tree was a big table with lots of chairs around it. But there were only three at the table: the Mad Hatter, the March **Hare** and a large brown mouse. The mouse sat between the Mad Hatter and the March Hare. It was asleep so they talked over its head.

When they saw Alice, they cried, 'No, no, you can't sit here! There isn't a **place** for you!'

'There are lots of places,' Alice said. She sat down in a chair at one end of the table.

'Have some **wine**,' the Mad Hatter said politely.

Alice looked round the table but there was only **tea**.

'I don't see any wine,' she answered.

'There isn't any,' said the March Hare.

'Then why did you say, "Have some wine"? It wasn't very **polite** of you,' Alice said angrily.

'We didn't invite you to tea but you came. That wasn't very polite of *you*,' said the March Hare.

'No, it wasn't. Cut your hair!' said the Mad Hatter.

'Oh, be quiet,' said Alice.

The Mad Hatter opened his eyes very **wide** but he didn't say a word. Then he took out his watch and looked at it. 'What day is it?' he asked.

Alice thought for a moment. 'Wednesday, I think,' she said.

'My watch says Monday,' the Mad Hatter said. 'You see, I was right. Butter isn't good for a watch.' He looked **angrily** at the March Hare.

'But it was the *best* butter,' answered the March Hare.

'Yes, but you put it on with the bread knife. Perhaps some bread got in.'

The March Hare took the watch from the Mad Hatter and looked at it sadly. Then he put it in his tea. He took it out and looked at it again. 'It was the *best* butter, you know,' he repeated.

Alice looked at the watch. 'It's a strange watch!' she said. 'It tells you the day but it doesn't tell you the time.'

'So, does your watch tell you the year?' asked the Mad Hatter.

'No,' Alice answered, 'but it's the same year for a very long time.'

'And my watch doesn't tell the time because it's always tea-time.'

2 Find and write.

1. _____angrily_____ the way you speak or act when something has made you unhappy or cross

2. _____ a big rabbit

3. _____ where you sit or stand

4. _____ this is when you say please and thank you

5. _____ a hot, brown drink

6. _____ open as much as possible

7. _____ a red or white drink for men or women

5a I can hear Claudia's voice.

1 **Listen and say. Then listen and read.** •))

 voice

 ribbon

 neck

 toes

 elbow

 knees

 tummy

Come here, pussy cat.

Owwwww!

Claudia: Come here, pussy cat. Come to Mummy.

Kelly: I can hear Claudia's voice.

Claudia: Magnus, tie this ribbon around the cat's neck. Then it can't run away.

Magnus: Whose cat is it?

Claudia: I don't know but it's my cat now.

Jack: Oh, no! They've got Oscar.

Suddenly Oscar ran past the children and into the next carriage.

Kelly: No, they haven't got Oscar.

Claudia: Magnus, find that cat!

Jack: He's coming this way. Quick! Hide!

Claudia: Ow!

Kelly: What happened, Jack? Did you see what happened?

Jack: Magnus stood on Claudia's toes. She's hopping up and down and waving her arms around.

Magnus: Ow!

Kelly: What was that, Jack? What happened this time?

Jack: Magnus tried to get past Claudia but she accidentally hit him with her elbow. Magnus is on his knees. He's holding his tummy.

Kelly: Let's go back to Aunt Sophie. We must find Oscar.

② Let's learn! Read.

Whose cat is it?
Oscar isn't Claudia's cat. He's Kelly and Jack's cat.

③ Read the story again, choose and write. Then match.

Oscar's   ~~Claudia's~~   Magnus's   Claudia's

1 Kelly heard ___Claudia's___   **a** tummy.
2 Magnus stood on _____   **b** neck.
3 Magnus tried to tie a ribbon around _____   **c** voice.
4 Claudia's elbow hit _____   **d** toes.

④ Listen and circle. Then point, ask and answer. •))

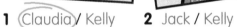

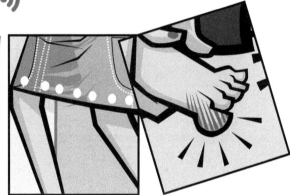

1 (Claudia) / Kelly   **2** Jack / Kelly   **3** Jack / Magnus   **4** Kelly / Aunt Sophie   **5** Dr Wild / Claudia

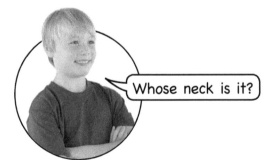
Whose neck is it?

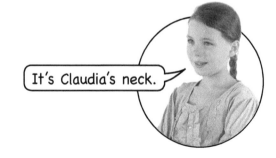
It's Claudia's neck.

⑤ Play the game.

Whose hand is it?

It's Adam's hand.

Is it yours?

1 Listen and say. Then listen and read. 🔊

scarf   glove   jacket   belt   trainers   tie   rescue

1 You're safe, Oscar. You're our cat, not theirs!

Now we must rescue Toto.

2 We're at the station. Oh, no! Look!

We must get off the train.

Here's your scarf, Aunt Sophie.

3 Look – a glove. Is it yours?

No, it isn't mine. Is it Claudia's?

Yes, it's hers.

4 This bag isn't ours. Whose is it?

I think it's Magnus's.

5 What's in it?

There are some clothes – a jacket and a belt.

6 Anything else?

Yes, there are some trainers and a tie.

That tie is definitely his.

2 Let's learn! Read.

I	mine
you	yours
he	his
she	hers
we	ours
they	theirs

Whose is it?

Whose are they?

It's mine.

They're yours.

3 Read the story again and match.

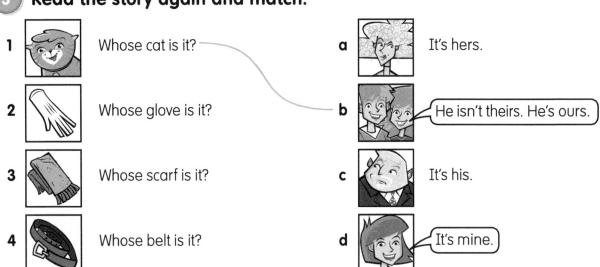

1 Whose cat is it?

2 Whose glove is it?

3 Whose scarf is it?

4 Whose belt is it?

a It's hers.

b He isn't theirs. He's ours.

c It's his.

d It's mine.

4 Look, ask and answer.

Kelly   Jack

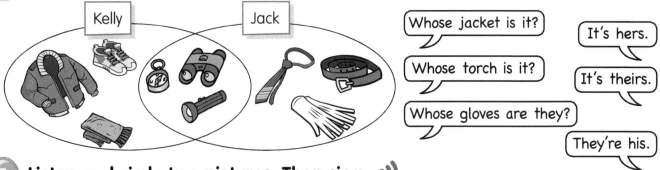

Whose jacket is it?

It's hers.

Whose torch is it?

It's theirs.

Whose gloves are they?

They're his.

5 Listen and circle two pictures. Then sing. •))

①

Whose scarf is this? It isn't mine.
Whose scarf is this? Do you know?
It's long and blue. It's got spots on, too.
It isn't hers. It isn't his. Is it yours?

Whose bag is this? It isn't ours.
Whose bag is this? Do you know?
It's big and new. It looks strong, too.
It isn't hers. It isn't his. Is it theirs?

③

②

④

5c You don't have to shout!

1 Listen and say. Then listen and read. •))

arrive

leave

start

lose

bring

finish

Kit: Is there an email from Jack and Kelly?

Mel: No, there isn't but they're online. We can talk to them.

Kit: Hello. Any news?

Mel: Kit, you don't have to shout! They can hear you.

Kelly: We're in Poland. We arrived this morning at half past ten.

Jack: Claudia and Magnus got off the train and we left the train quickly.

Kelly: Magnus dropped his bag. We started to follow but we lost them. We left the bag at the station.

Mel: Have they got Toto?

Kelly: Yes, they brought Toto with them.

Jack: We have to go now. Oscar is hungry and Kelly has to feed him. Then we must go to bed. We have to get up early and look for Toto. We think Claudia and Magnus want to go to Ukraine tomorrow.

Mel: Yes, and I have to do my homework.

Kelly: It's very late.

Kit: It's OK. She doesn't have to finish it tonight.

Jack: That's good.

Mel: Bye.

2 Read the story again and write True or False.

1 Kelly and Jack are in Poland. __True__

2 They arrived at half past nine. _____

3 Claudia and Magnus stayed on the train. _____

4 Kelly and Jack lost Claudia and Magnus. _____

5 Claudia and Magnus brought Toto with them. _____

6 Kit has got some homework to do. _____

3 Let's learn! Read.

I/You/We/They
We have to look after Oscar.
I don't have to feed him.
They have to look for Toto.
They don't have to start looking tonight.

He/She/It
Kelly has to feed him.
She doesn't have to brush him. I do.

4 Look and say.

1 tidy the bedroom

2 get up early

3 feed the dog

4 walk to school

5 do homework

6 wear a uniform

Picture 1: They have to tidy the bedroom.
Picture 2: He doesn't have to get up early.

5 Choose and write.

bring   finishes   ~~leave~~   start   arrive

Every day I have to (1) _____leave_____ home at eight o'clock. I (2) _____ at school at half past eight. My lessons (3) _____ at nine o'clock. I don't have to (4) _____ my lunch to school; I can eat in the canteen. School (5) _____ at three o'clock.

6 Think and write with Dr Wild.

get up early   go shopping   help my mum and dad   wear a uniform
go to school   do my homework   make my bed   tidy my room   feed the cat

Imagine it's Monday. What do you have to do today?

I have to get up early.
I don't have to go shopping.
_____
_____
_____
_____
_____

59

5d

SKILLS

I arrive at twenty to nine.

1 **Look and say what Beth, Kit, Harry and Mel do at these times.**

> Picture 1: Beth rides her bike to school at ten past eight.

My school day

Every day I walk to school. It isn't very far. I leave my house at half past eight and I arrive at ten to nine.

Our first lesson starts at five to nine. We stop for lunch at quarter past twelve. I bring a lunch box from home. We don't have to bring a lunch box; we can eat lunch in the canteen.

After lunch I play with my friends in the playground. Lessons start again at one o'clock. School finishes at ten past three. Sometimes I have lessons after school. On Mondays I have a guitar lesson at quarter to four. On Thursdays I have a swimming lesson at half past five. Some days I have to go shopping with my mum.

2 **Read the homework. Tick the correct picture.**

3 **Read again and match.**

1 My first lesson starts. ___b___
2 We finish school. _____
3 I have a guitar lesson. _____
4 I have a swimming lesson. _____

Writing class: AB, page 58

4 Listen and match. •))

① Kit ② Harry ③ Mel ④ Beth

ⓐ ⓑ ⓒ ⓓ

5 Listen again and draw. •))

After-school activities		
Place	**Activity**	**Time**
1 Music room	Guitar lesson	
2 Playing field	Football match	
3 Swimming pool	Swimming lesson	
4 School hall	Dance lesson	

6 Choose places and activities from 5 and write. Then act it out.

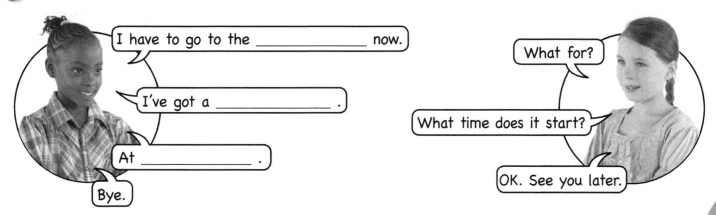

I have to go to the _____ now.

I've got a _____ .

At _____ .

Bye.

What for?

What time does it start?

OK. See you later.

History

1 Choose and write to complete the timeline.

21st   seventeenth   16th   14th   ~~eleventh~~   twentieth

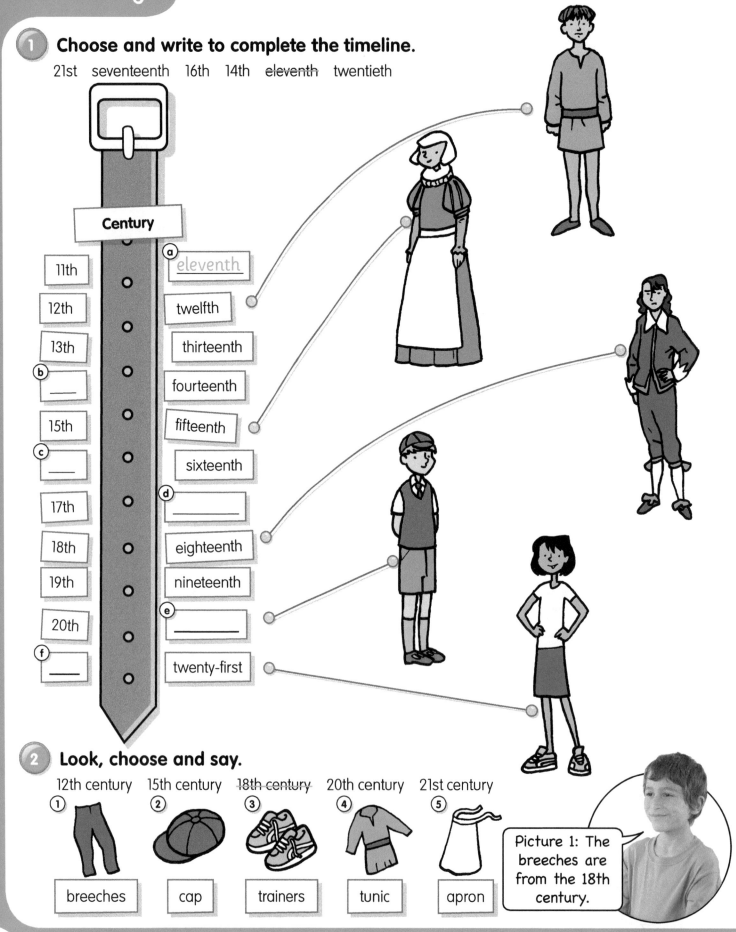

Century

11th	(a) _eleventh_
12th	twelfth
13th	thirteenth
(b) ___	fourteenth
15th	fifteenth
(c) ___	sixteenth
17th	(d) _____
18th	eighteenth
19th	nineteenth
20th	(e) _____
(f) ___	twenty-first

2 Look, choose and say.

12th century	15th century	~~18th century~~	20th century	21st century
①	②	③	④	⑤
breeches	cap	trainers	tunic	apron

Picture 1: The breeches are from the 18th century.

62

3 Read and check.

For hundreds of years children's clothes in Europe didn't change much. Clothes stayed the same from the 5th to the 12th century. Boys in the 12th century wore a short tunic with a belt and trousers. Girls wore trousers with a long dress on top.

From the 14th century girls wore a dress with a belt and a cap on their head. They often wore aprons to keep their dresses clean. Boys wore a shirt, a belt, trousers and boots or shoes. Poor children didn't always have shoes.

From the 16th to the 18th century children wore the same clothes as men and women. The girls wore long dresses. The boys wore dresses too until they were seven years old. Then they wore a shirt, a jacket and short trousers called breeches, with long socks and shoes. Until the end of the 19th century most children had only one new dress or shirt a year.

After 1900 there were many different **fashions**. The boy wearing a **school uniform** lived in the 20th century. The 21st century girl is wearing **casual** clothes.

4 Read again and answer.

1 Did fashion change much from the 5th to the 12th century? _No, it didn't._

2 When did boys wear a short tunic with a belt and trousers? _____

3 Did girls and women wear the same fashion in the 17th century? _____

4 How old were boys when they wore trousers in the 18th century? _____

5 How many new dresses did girls have a year in the 19th century? _____

6 Did fashion change much in the 20th century? _____

5 Your project! Draw and write about your favourite clothes.

My favourite clothes are a skirt and a T-shirt. My favourite skirt is white and my favourite T-shirt is blue with a picture of a horse on it. My mum and dad gave me the T-shirt for my birthday because I like horses. I wear these clothes when I go to parties.

6a The red van is better!

1 Listen and say. Then listen and read. 🔊

van

motorbike

fire engine

scooter

helicopter

1 The white van is bigger than the red one.

The red one is smaller but it's better.

The red van, please!

2 Claudia and Magnus are on a motorbike!

Yes. It's faster than our van!

Go faster, Aunt Sophie!

3 Be careful! There's a fire engine behind us!

There's a scooter in front! Go slower, Aunt Sophie!

4 They're stopping!

Good. We're at the airport. There are lots of helicopters.

5 No, they're getting into the older one.

Are they getting into the new helicopter?

6 I'm a pilot. Come on. We need a helicopter, too!

Name: Sophie Wild
Age: 30
Hair: Brown
Nationality: British

PILOT

Home Town: Bristol
Hobbies: Flying planes, reading, sport

2 Let's learn! Read.

old	older
big	bigger
happy	happier
good	better
bad	worse

The yellow helicopter is older than the green one.

3 Read the story again and write True or False.

1 The red van is smaller than the white one. ___True___

2 The white van is better than the red one. _____

3 The van is faster than the motorbike. _____

4 The motorbike is smaller than the van. _____

5 The yellow helicopter is dirtier than the green one. _____

6 The green helicopter is newer than the yellow one. _____

4 Listen and tick the correct picture. Then look, choose and write ·))

GREAT TRANSPORT RACE

1 small/big   The fire engine is _____bigger_____ than the ambulances.

2 dirty/clean   The black van is _____ than the white one.

3 slow/fast   The green motorbike is _____ than the yellow one.

4 tall/short   The man is _____ than the woman.

5 happy/slow   The woman is _____ than the man

5 Look at the pictures in 4. Say and guess.

I can see three vans and a scooter.

Picture a.

1 Listen and say. Then listen and read. ◑))

 runner   catch   silly   heavy   noisy   light

Where are you, Kelly? What are you doing now?

We're in a helicopter. We're following Claudia and Magnus!

Kelly: We didn't catch Claudia and Magnus at the airport.

Beth: Jack is the fastest runner in our school!

Kelly: Yes, but they got in their helicopter first. But I think they're the silliest people in the world. They didn't choose the fastest one! They chose the slowest, heaviest, oldest, noisiest one. Aunt Sophie is a pilot and we got the fastest, lightest and quietest helicopter.

Beth: Can you see Toto?

Kelly: Yes! I think he's the saddest bird in the world at the moment. We have to catch Claudia and Magnus! It's amazing up here. We can see the River Danube.

Beth: Is that the longest river in Europe?

Harry: No, the Volga is longer.

Beth: How's Oscar?

Kelly: He's really happy. He thinks he's a helicopter pilot. He's the funniest cat I know!

2 Read the story again and circle.

1 He runs very fast.   **a** Jack   **b** Magnus

2 They're very silly.   **a** Oscar and Toto   **b** Claudia and Magnus

3 It's old and heavy.   **a** the green helicopter   **b** the yellow helicopter

4 He's very sad.   **a** Toto   **b** Oscar

5 It's very long.   **a** the green helicopter   **b** the river

3 Let's learn! Read.

fast	the fastest
big	the biggest
noisy	the noisiest
good	the best
bad	the worst

Jack is the fastest runner I know!

4 Choose and write.

runner   heavy   noisy   light   ~~silly~~

1 I don't like clowns. I think they're ___silly___ .

2 She's a good _____ . She came first in the race at school.

3 My school bag has got ten books in it. It's really _____ .

4 I haven't got any books in my bag. It's _____ .

5 My brother is playing the drums. I can't hear you. It's very _____ !

5 Write and match. Then ask and answer.

1 high   The ___highest___ mountain is   **a** Vatican City.

2 long   The _____ river is   **b** Mount Everest.

3 fast   The _____ animal is   **c** Russia.

4 big   The _____ animal is   **d** the cheetah.

5 small The _____ country is   **e** the Nile.

6 big   The _____ country is   **f** the blue whale.

What's the highest mountain in the world?

Mount Everest.

6 Listen, choose and write. Then sing.

sweeter   ~~cleverest~~   bigger   funnier   faster   cleverest

He's a little bit lazy and a little bit fat

But we think Oscar is the (1) ___cleverest___ cat!

Other cats are (2) _____ , they run (3) _____ , too

But other cats can't do what Oscar can do.

He's (4) _____ than them and he's (5) _____ , too.

He always makes us laugh when we're sad and blue.

He's a little bit silly and he can't catch mice

But we don't mind because we think he's very nice.

He's a little bit lazy and a little bit fat

But we think Oscar is the (6) _____ cat!

Oscar has got the softest bed!

1 Listen and say. Then listen and read. •))

 tobogganing
 rich
 cheap
 dark
 soft
 hard
 easy

Kelly: What a beautiful place!

They were in the mountains and there was lots of snow.

Jack: Where are we now?

Dr Wild: We're in Ukraine. Where are Claudia and Magnus?

Jack: They went into that hotel. It's bigger than ours.

Dr Wild: Yes, it's the biggest in the town. They're richer than us. This hotel is cheaper than theirs.

Jack: I think this hotel is better. There's a computer in every room.

Kelly: The rooms are nicer. The rooms in that hotel look darker.

Jack: I want this bed. It's softer than the others. I don't like hard beds.

Dr Wild: Look at Oscar. He's got the softest bed!

Kelly: Look at those people skiing. They're having fun.

Jack: I like tobogganing better. It's easier than skiing. Tobogganing is safer, too.

2 Let's learn! Read.

cheap	cheaper	the cheapest
good	better	the best
bad	worse	the worst

Kelly's bed is soft. Jack's bed is softer. My bed is the softest!

3 Read the story again and write True or False.

1 Dr Wild is richer than Claudia and Magnus. ___False___
2 Hotel Posh is the cheapest hotel in the town. _____
3 Hotel Posh is darker than Hotel Trendy. _____
4 Kelly's bed is the softest. _____
5 Tobogganing is easier than skiing. _____

4 Look, choose and write.

hard ~~easy~~ new cheap

1 Tobogganing is ___easier___ than skiing.
   Walking is ___the easiest___ .
2 The car is _____ than the motorbike.
   The scooter is _____ .
3 The red chair is _____ than the blue one.
   The brown chair is _____ .
4 The blue phone is _____ than the black one.
   The purple phone is _____ .

5 Think and write with Dr Wild.

fastest noisiest cheapest safest worst easiest best

Think about different sports and write.

I think motorbike racing is the noisiest sport.
_____
_____
_____
_____
_____

1 Look and say.

wheel   gears   handlebars   brake   saddle

> I like the blue bike. It's got lots of gears and the smallest handlebars.

COME TO CYCLE WORLD

ONLY €210

18

Red Storm

ONLY €450

27

King of the Road

Sunny Friend

ONLY €99.99

6

(1) _Sunny Friend_ is the biggest bike in the shop. It isn't the fastest bike but it's the easiest to ride with a nice, big, black saddle and handlebars – and a fabulous big basket for all your books!

(2) _____ is the lightest bike we've got. It's brilliant! It's got a blue saddle and with 27 gears it's the fastest bike in the shop. With this bike you can go faster than all your friends!

Do you want a really amazing bike? Then (3) _____ is for you! This fantastic small red bike has got stronger brakes than all the others and better and bigger lights, too. It's not the cheapest bike in the shop but we think it's the best!

2 Read and complete with the names of the bikes.

3 Look, read and answer.

1 Which bike is the cheapest? _Sunny Friend_

2 Which bike is the fastest? _____

3 Which bike is the easiest to ride? _____

4 Which bike has got the strongest brakes? _____

5 Which bike has got the biggest lights? _____

6 Which bike is the lightest? _____

SALE SALE SALE SALE
DESIRABLE TRAINERS
BUY NOW-PRICES BELOW!

€87

€45

€215

€150

4 Look and write the prices in words.

1 The pink trainers are _____forty-five_____ euros.
2 The yellow trainers are _____ euros.
3 The purple trainers are _____ euros.
4 The white trainers are _____ euros.

5 Listen, circle and write. •))

Mel thinks …

1 the yellow / pink ones are the easiest to put on.
2 the white / yellow ones are the coolest.
3 the purple / white ones are the strongest.
4 the yellow / purple ones are the biggest and highest.
5 she can only buy the _____ ones.

6 Choose and write. Then act it out.

better   cheaper   stronger   cooler   smaller   bigger   lighter

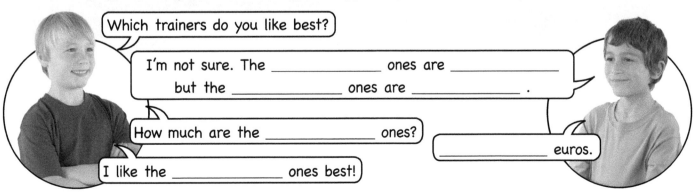

Which trainers do you like best?

I'm not sure. The _____ ones are _____ but the _____ ones are _____ .

How much are the _____ ones?

_____ euros.

I like the _____ ones best!

Science

1 Look and guess.

1 What are the names of the planets?
2 Which is the hottest?
3 Which is the coldest?
4 Which is the smallest?
5 Which is the biggest?

Did you know that the sun is a very big, very hot star? It gives lots of energy to nine planets and those planets are in our solar system.

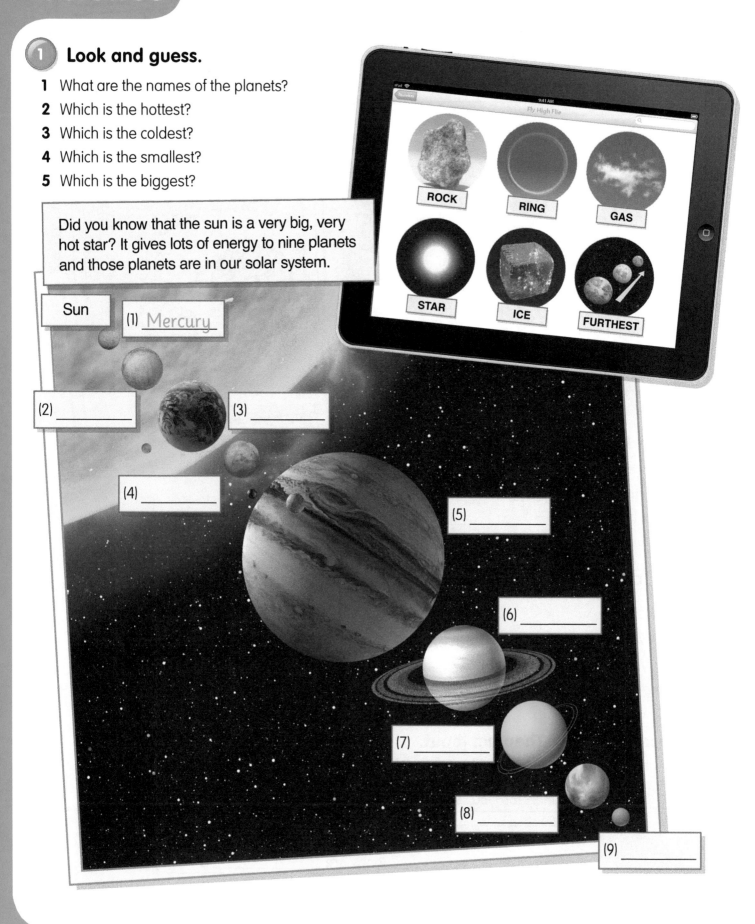

ROCK

RING

GAS

STAR

ICE

FURTHEST

Sun

(1) Mercury

(2) _____

(3) _____

(4) _____

(5) _____

(6) _____

(7) _____

(8) _____

(9) _____

2 **Read and check. Then label the planets in 1.**

The planet nearest to the sun is Mercury. It's the fastest planet. It goes around the sun very quickly. But it isn't the hottest planet. Venus is the hottest planet and it's second nearest to the sun. The third planet is Earth, where you and I live! The next planet is Mars. It's smaller than Earth.

The first four planets are made of rock. Next to Mars is the biggest planet, Jupiter. It's made of gas, not rock. Jupiter hasn't got one moon like Earth, it's got 16 large moons and many small ones.

Saturn has got more than 60 moons! It's the sixth furthest planet from the sun and there are many colourful rings around it. They're rings of ice! Next is Uranus. It's four times bigger than Earth. Then comes Neptune. It's blue and beautiful. There are often storms on Neptune. The last planet, furthest from the sun, is Pluto. Pluto is the smallest planet. It's smaller than our moon and it's the coldest planet, too. Some people think Pluto isn't a planet because it's very small.

3 **Read again and write the name of the planet.**

Which planet ...

1 is nearest to the sun? _Mercury_

2 is second nearest to the sun? _____

3 is furthest from the sun? _____

4 is the fastest? _____

5 is the stormiest? _____

6 has got many colourful rings? _____

4 **Your project!** **Choose a planet and write about it.**

	Jupiter	Venus	Neptune
Made of	gas	rock	gas
Temperature	very cold	hot	very cold
Other information	16 moons	cloudy	very stormy

Neptune is a beautiful blue planet. It's made of gas and it's very cold. It's very stormy.

73

Review 3

1 **Look, choose and write.**

elbow   ~~toes~~   tummy   neck   knees

1 _____ They're Ben's toes. _____

2 _____ It's _____

3 _____

4 _____

5 _____

Ben   Millie

2 **Listen and match.** •))

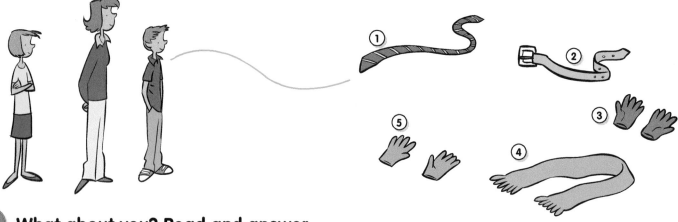

3 **What about you? Read and answer.**

1 Is your hair longer than your teacher's? _____

2 Is your school bag heavier than your friend's? _____

3 Are your shoes bigger than your friend's? _____

4 Is your class noisier than the class next to yours? _____

4 **Listen and chant.** •))

I know a ghost on an island.
He climbs up the castle at night!

5 Play the game. = move one space = move two spaces

Start
1

Who's the tallest person?
1 point
2

Find and say three parts of the body.
3 points
3

Whose knees can you see?
1 point
4

– 2 points
5

Well done!
20

Who's leaving the shop?
1 point
6

What is higher than the town hall?
1 point
19

Find and say three numbers.
3 points
7

Which is darker: the car or the van?
1 point
18

What time is it?
1 point
8

2 points
17

2 points
9

Does the police officer have to wear a uniform?
1 point
16

Who's furthest from the clothes shop?
1 point
10

Find and say three things you can ride.
3 points
15

How many elbows can you see?
1 point
14

– 2 points
13

Whose van is it?
1 point
12

Find and say three things that are cheaper than the scarf.
3 points
11

The Prince and the Pauper

1 **Read and listen.** •))

PENGUIN READERS

The Prince and the Pauper

Mark Twain

Every day Tom went to the palace where the king of England lived. Tom was **poor** and he **beg**ged on the way and sometimes got money. More often he got a kick.

Then one day Tom saw a boy in the palace. He looked at the boy's beautiful clothes and he knew. It was Prince Edward, the king's son! He ran to the doors.

'I want to see the prince,' he cried.

One of the **soldiers** hit Tom. Tom fell and they all laughed. But the prince saw and was very angry.

'Why did you hit that poor boy?' he shouted at the soldiers. 'Open the doors. Bring him in.'

'But sir … ,' said the soldier. 'He's only a poor, dirty **beggar**.'

'My father is king of rich people and poor people,' answered Prince Edward. 'Bring in the boy.'

The prince took Tom inside the palace, up some stairs and into one of his rooms.

'Are you hungry?' he asked.

'I'm always hungry, sir,' answered Tom.

Edward called a **servant**.

'Bring some food,' he ordered. 'Meat, cake, fruit and bread.'

The servant brought food and Tom ate.

'Now, who are you?' asked the prince. 'I see you near the palace every day. I watch you from the window.'

'My name is Tom Canty, sir. I live with my family in a room near London Bridge.'

'In a room?'

'Yes – with my mother, my father, my grandmother and my two sisters. Our room is quite big and it's very cheap.'

'Why do you all live in one room?'

'Because we're very poor,' said Tom. 'My father doesn't work and I have to beg for money.'

'I have two sisters, too, but they don't play with me and I don't know any boys. Do you play with other boys?'

'Yes, of course. We play by the river and we swim. Sometimes we play princes and soldiers. I'm always the prince,' said Tom.

Edward was sad. 'I would like to be a poor boy,' he said. 'I would like to play with other boys.'

Then Edward had an idea. He jumped out of his chair. 'Let's change clothes. You can be the prince and I can be the **pauper**.'

Edward put on Tom's old thin trousers and shirt. Tom washed his face and hands. They had the same eyes, the same nose, the same hair. Tom put on Edward's fine clothes and shoes.

'Wait here!' said the prince. 'I want to be a pauper for a day. I'm going to the river to swim.'

He ran out of the room.

'What do I do now?' shouted Tom.

But there was no answer.

2 Find and write.

1.  ___beg___
to ask a person you don't know for money

2. _____
this person asks for money

3.  _____
a person who has little or no money

4.  _____
a person with little money is this

5.  _____
a person who works in the house of a king or queen

6.  _____
these people fight for their country

1 **Listen and say. Then listen and read.** •))

 fancy dress
 costume
 alien
 superhero
 pop star
 join in

2 Let's learn! Read.

I/You/We/They	He/She/It
I want to go tobogganing.	He wants to go fast.

3 Read the story again and match.

1 They want to find
2 Kelly wants to wear
3 She wants to be
4 Jack wants to be
5 They want to join
6 Oscar wants to go

a tobogganing.
b a superhero.
c in the fun.
d a pop star.
e Claudia and Magnus.
f a costume.

4 Listen and match. Then write.

1

2

3

4

Mel wants to be an _____alien_____ .

Harry wants to be a _____ .

Beth wants to be a _____ .

Kit wants to be a _____ .

5 Look, ask and answer.

have a drink   make a phone call   ~~go tobogganing~~   eat an ice cream   take the cat home   take photos

What does Oscar want to do?

He wants to go tobogganing.

He likes tobogganing!

1 Listen and say. Then listen and read. •))

 ice skating   surfing   skateboarding   rock climbing   cycling   fishing

① Kit

②

③

④

Beth: We got some more photos from Kelly and Jack yesterday.	**Beth:** You like skateboarding and rollerblading, too.
Mel: There's a funny photo of Oscar on a toboggan.	**Mel:** True.
Kit: He's the funniest cat in the world! He likes tobogganing!	**Harry:** I like climbing. I'm happy when I'm climbing trees.
Beth: I like tobogganing, too. It's fun. I love winter sports. I like skiing and ice skating, too.	**Beth:** Do you like rock climbing, too, Harry?
Mel: You're good at ice skating, Beth.	**Harry:** Yes, I do but it's difficult. What about you, Kit?
Beth: Thank you.	**Kit:** I like cycling and fishing. Last weekend I went to the mountains with my dad. We went cycling in the morning and fishing in the afternoon. I caught a bicycle wheel! I'm not very good at fishing.
Mel: I like going to the beach. I enjoy swimming and surfing.	

2 Read the story again and write the names.

3 Let's learn! Read.

Oscar likes tobogganing.
He enjoys climbing trees.
He's good at making friends.
He's happy when he's playing with Jack and Kelly.

4 Look, ask and answer. Then ask and answer about you.

Does Kit like playing basketball?

Does Mel enjoy swimming?

No, he doesn't.

Yes, she does.

5 Look, circle and write.

1 She is / isn't good at ___skateboarding___ .   3 He is / isn't good at _____ .

2 She is / isn't good at _____ .   4 He is / isn't good at _____ .

6 Listen, choose and write. Then sing.

sleeping   drinking   morning   head   ~~eating~~

I'm happy when I'm (1) _eating_
a lovely juicy fish.
I'm happy when I'm (2) _____
milk from my dish.
I'm happy when I'm (3) _____
in my comfortable bed.

I'm happy when somebody
is stroking my (4) _____
I'm happy in the (5) _____
and in the evening, too.
But most of all I'm happy
when I'm with you.

7c What shall we do?

1 Listen and say. Then listen and read. •))

 use
 escape
 reach
 borrow
 hold

Jack: Oh, no! Did you see? Magnus was the alien! Claudia was the spy!

Kelly: They've got Oscar!

Jack: What shall we do now? They're halfway down the mountain.

Dr Wild: We have to rescue Oscar.

Jack: What about using the helicopter?

Dr Wild: No time for that! They're escaping! We must stop them before they reach the town.

Kelly: What about skiing after them?

Dr Wild: I'm not very good at skiing.

Kelly: Shall we ask the other people to help?

Dr Wild: Yes! That's a good idea.

Kelly: Excuse me, can you help us? That man and woman have got our cat! We have to catch them.

Man: That's terrible. You can borrow our toboggan.

Jack: Thank you.

Man: Shall I hold it for you?

Kelly: Yes. Thank you.

Dr Wild: Are we all on?

Kelly: Yes, we are.

Dr Wild: Off we go! Everybody to the rescue!

2 Let's learn! Read.

Help! What shall I do? Shall I jump off?

Oh, no! What shall we do? What about using the helicopter?

3 Read the story again, circle and match.

1 What shall we (do) / doing — d
2 What about use / using
3 What about ski / skiing
4 Shall we ask / asking
5 Shall I hold / holding

a the helicopter?
b the toboggan for you?
c the other people to help?
d now?
e after Claudia and Magnus?

4 Read and circle.

Look, Claudia. Those children are following us. They're (1) (using) / doing a toboggan. They want to (2) ask / rescue the cat. What shall we do?

Go faster. I'm (3) stopping / holding the cat and it can't (4) rescue / escape! We must (5) reach / catch the town before they do and hide. Then tonight we can (6) help / borrow a car and drive away.

5 Think and write with Dr Wild.

play football/tennis/basketball/volleyball/computer games
go to the swimming pool/park/cinema/for a walk/watch TV/listen to music/make a cake

Think about what you can do at the weekend. Write suggestions for your friend.

Hi,
I've got some ideas for this weekend.
Shall we play football on Saturday morning?
_____
_____
_____

Shall we meet in the park or at my house?

1 Look at the pictures and say.

Picture 1: Play football.

To: Kit@yazoo.com

From: Harry@yazoo.com

Subject: Where shall we meet?

Hi Kit,

Thanks for your email. I'm very excited that you can come and stay for the weekend.
Shall we meet in the park or at my house?
We can have lunch at my house. What shall we do after lunch? Do you want to play football or go fishing? I know you like fishing and there's a lake near my house. You can use my dad's fishing rod and I can borrow one from my friend. In the evening we can watch a film or what about playing computer games? I've got the Winter Games Wii. I like playing the ice skating game but I'm not very good at it.
Have you got any DVDs or computer games? Can you bring them with you, please?

See you soon.

Harry

① ✓ ② ③

④ ⑤ ⑥ ⑦

2 Read and tick the activities in the email.

3 Read again and circle.

1 Kit can come and stay for   **a** Saturday and Sunday.   **b** the week.

2 They can have lunch   **a** at Kit's house.   **b** at Harry's house.

3 Harry wants Kit to bring   **a** the Winter Games Wii.   **b** some DVDs.

4 Listen and number.))

5 Listen again and circle. Then write.))

1 Kit wants to go _rollerblading_ today.

2 Harry wants to go _____ today.

3 Mel wants to go _____ today.

6 Choose a holiday and activities from 4 and write. Then act it out.

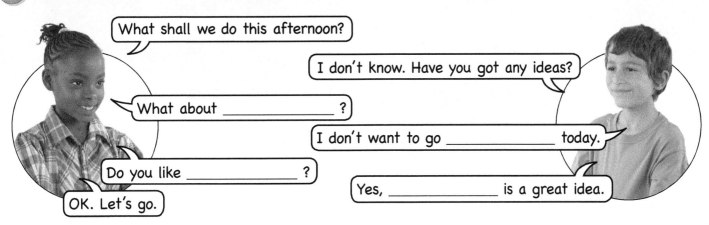

What shall we do this afternoon?

I don't know. Have you got any ideas?

What about _____ ?

I don't want to go _____ today.

Do you like _____ ?

Yes, _____ is a great idea.

OK. Let's go.

This is **Lionel Messi**. He's one of the best football players in the world.

He **scores** a **goal** nearly every game.

GOAL!

This is **Michael Phelps**. He's one of the best swimmers in history.

Olympic flag

gold medal

He holds the **world record** for 100 metres butterfly. It's 49.82 seconds.

1 Look, read and guess.

1 Who eats eight eggs, cheese, toast, pancakes and cereal for breakfast?

2 Who lives in Spain?

3 Who needed medicine to grow when he was 11 years old?

4 Who has got very big feet?

2 Read and check.

Lionel Messi always wanted to be a football player. He was born in Argentina in 1987 and he played for his first team when he was five years old.

By 11 he was very good at football but there was a problem. He was short and he wasn't growing. He needed medicine to grow but it wasn't cheap. When he was 13, his family moved to Spain and the Barcelona football club paid for his medicine.

Today he plays for FC Barcelona and Argentina. He's a brilliant goal scorer and one of the best football players in the world.

Michael Phelps is an amazing American swimmer. When he was 15, he **competed** in the 2000 Olympics and the next year he broke a world record. He's got 14 Olympic gold medals. He wants to win more medals so he works very hard. Every day he swims for about five hours.

He's tall with a long body and big feet and he eats very big meals. He eats the same as five men every day. He loves his sport and he's happy when he's swimming.

3 Read again and answer.

1 Where was Lionel Messi born? __Argentina__

2 How old is he? _____

3 How did Barcelona help him? _____

4 What teams does he play for? _____

5 What nationality is Michael Phelps? _____

6 What did he do when he was 15 years old? _____

7 How many Olympic gold medals has he got? _____

8 How much does he eat every day? _____

4 Your project! Find out and write about a sporting legend from your country.

I love skiing and I'm good at it. In the winter I go with my family to the mountains and we ski every day. I want to be as good as Justyna Kowalczyk. She's a Polish skier. She won three medals in the 2010 Winter Olympics. I want to win lots of medals, too.

1 Listen and say. Then listen and read. •))

lamp   curtain   rug   sofa   cushion   prison   knock over

2 Let's learn! Read.

I
I'm going to look upstairs.

He/She/It
She's going to call the police.

We/You/They
They're going to go to prison.

I'm going to hide!

3 Read the story again and correct one word.

1 Dr Wild is going to help the police. ___phone___

2 Jack is going to sleep upstairs. _____

3 Claudia and Kelly are behind the curtains. _____

4 Toto is playing behind a cushion. _____

5 Claudia and Magnus are going to go to school. _____

4 Listen and circle. Then choose and write.

to wash   to paint   to clean   to make

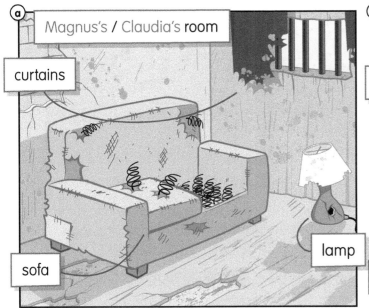

a Magnus's / Claudia's **room**

curtains

sofa

lamp

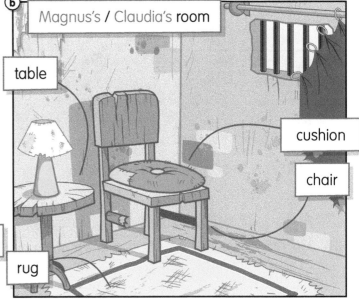

b Magnus's / Claudia's **room**

table

cushion

chair

rug

1 Magnus ___is___ going ___to clean___ his room.

2 He _____ going _____ some new curtains.

3 Claudia _____ going _____ the rug.

4 She _____ going _____ the lamp.

5 Look and say.

Oscar is going to drink some milk.

①

drink some milk

②

phone Sally at the zoo

③

email their friends

④ **You?**

1 **Listen and say. Then listen and read.** •))

picnic

invitation

banner

plan

send

Harry: Jack and Kelly have got Toto!

Kit: That's great!

Mel: Are they going to come home now?

Harry: Yes, they are but they aren't going to travel by train.

Kit: Are they going to fly home?

Harry: Yes, I think so.

Kit: Is Dr Wild going to take Toto to the zoo?

Harry: Yes, she is. Shall we have a party for them?

Mel: Yes! Let's plan a big picnic!

Harry: Yes, let's have a picnic. We can go to the park, take lots of food and then play games. Good idea!

Kit: Are you going to make a cake, Beth?

Beth: Yes, I am! I'm going to make a big chocolate cake!

Kit: I'm going to send invitations to all our friends.

Beth: I'm going to make a Welcome Home banner!

2 **Read the story again and write** True **or** False.

1 Jack and Kelly are going to go home. ___True___

2 They are going to travel by train. _____

3 Dr Wild is going to take Toto to the zoo. _____

4 Harry and his friends are going to plan a party for Jack and Kelly. _____

5 Mel is going to send invitations to all their friends. _____

6 Beth is going to make a cake and a banner. _____

③ Let's learn! Read.

I	He/She/It	We/You/They
Am I going to see my friends again? Yes, I am.	Is he going to fly home? Yes, he is.	Are they going to go by train? No, they aren't.
I'm not going to go to school.	He isn't going to go by train.	They aren't going to fly in a plane.

Are we going to go home now?

I'm not going to travel by train!

Yes, we are.

④ Write Yes or No for you. Then ask and answer.

What are you going to do this evening?

Are you going to watch TV this evening?

No, I'm not. I'm going to read a book.

⑤ Look, circle and write.

~~have~~ make eat drink write make

1 They **are** / aren't going to ___have___ a picnic.
2 The boy is / isn't going to _____ a banner.
3 The girl is / isn't going to _____ a cake.
4 Dad is / isn't going to _____ invitations.
5 They are / aren't going to _____ sandwiches.
6 They are / aren't going to _____ milk.

⑥ Listen and circle. Then sing. 🔊

Are you going to (1) **come** / be to our party?
It's going to (2) look / be just great.
We're going to (3) make / have a picnic.
Please come and don't be late!

We're going to (4) get / make some pizza.
We've got lots of (5) things / work to do.
It's going to (6) be / have such wonderful fun
And Toto is going to (7) fly / come, too!

Why did they want Toto?

1 **Listen and say. Then listen and read.**

 robber
 jewellery
 painting
 diamond
 steal
 rare
 valuable

Policeman: Claudia and Magnus are going to go to prison. They aren't going to come out for a long time!

Dr Wild: Why did they want Toto and Oscar, Officer?

Policeman: Because Claudia collects rare birds and she liked Oscar!

Kelly: Why didn't they buy a cat and a toucan?

Policewoman: Because Claudia and Magnus are robbers.

Policeman: They never buy anything, they always steal things. We found lots of jewellery and valuable paintings in their house in Switzerland.

Policewoman: There were lots of valuable diamonds, too!

Dr Wild: Thank you for your help, Officer.

Policeman: Thank you, Dr Wild, and thank you, Kelly and Jack. You were very brave and helpful.

Dr Wild: Now we must go home.

Jack: Yes! We can't wait to see Mel, Harry, Beth and Kit.

② Let's learn! Read.

Why did Claudia want me and Toto? Because she liked us!

Why didn't we like Claudia? Because she was a robber!

③ Read the story again and match.

1 Why aren't Claudia and Magnus in the hotel?   **a** Because they were brave and helpful.
2 Why did Claudia want Toto?   **b** Because they're going to go to prison.
3 Why did she want Oscar?   **c** Because they're robbers.
4 Why didn't they buy some animals?   **d** Because she collects rare birds.
5 Why did the policeman thank Kelly and Jack?   **e** Because she liked him.

④ Look, choose and write.

paintings   valuable   ~~robbers~~   diamonds   jewellery   stealing

This is Magnus and Claudia's house. Why did the police in Switzerland go there? Because they knew Claudia and Magnus were (1) _____robbers_____ !
They found many (2) _____ things there.
Under the bed there was a big bag of
(3) _____ . In the cupboard there was lots of
(4) _____ and there were two
(5) _____ in front of the bed. They liked
(6) _____ !

⑤ Think and write with Dr Wild.

Think about your favourite hobby. Tick the things you like about it and write.

I like swimming because I'm good at it and I like sport.

_____
_____
_____
_____
_____

I can do it with my friends. _____   I like sport. _____   I get lots of fresh air. _____
I can do it at home. _____   I like collecting things. _____   I wear special clothes. _____
I can do it on my own. _____   I'm happy when I'm doing it. _____   I'm good at it. _____
I can do it at the weekends. _____   It's good fun. _____   I learn lots of new things. _____

8d
SKILLS

Would you like to come to our party?

1 Look and answer.

Who's the invitation from?   Who's the email from?

I've got an invitation from Kit!

WOULD YOU LIKE TO COME TO OUR
PARTY?

To Roz

The occasion: A Welcome Home picnic for Jack and Kelly

The time: 3.00 in the afternoon

The date: Saturday August 8th

The place: Greenwoods Park

RSVP Tel: Kit 7855021   Email: kit@yazoo.com

To: Kit@yazoo.com

From: Roz@yazoo.com

Subject: Party Invitation!

Dear Kit,

Thank you for the invitation to the Welcome Home picnic for Jack and Kelly. I'd love to come. I can't wait to see them and hear all their news. The last time I saw them was on May 22nd and it's August 3rd now! Would you like me to bring some food and drink to the picnic? I can bring some sandwiches, crisps and juice.

Love Roz

2 Read and answer.

1 What's the occasion?

   A Welcome Home picnic for Jack and Kelly

2 Where's the party?

   _____

3 What time is it?

   _____

4 Is Roz going to go?

   _____

5 What's she going to take to the picnic?

   _____

Writing class: AB, page 92

3 Listen and circle. •))

	1	2	3
Occasion	(Birthday party) Fancy dress party	Birthday party Fancy dress party	Picnic School dance
Date	Saturday September 15th Saturday September 5th	Friday October 31st Friday October 3rd	Wednesday March 5th Wednesday March 25th
Time	7.30 5.30	3.45 4.15	7.30 5.30
Place	Peter's house the park	the school Tom's house	the school Kate's house

4 Choose a party from 3 and complete.

WOULD YOU LIKE TO COME TO MY

PARTY?

To ....

The
occasion: ....

The time: ....

The date: ....

The place: ....

RSVP Tel: .... Email: ....

5 Write. Then act it out.

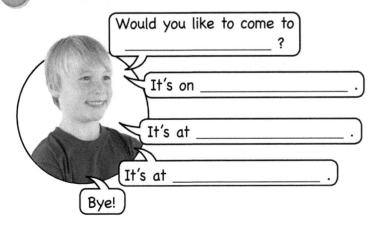

Would you like to come to _____ ?

It's on _____ .

It's at _____ .

It's at _____ .

Bye!

Thank you. Yes, I'd love to come. When is it?

What time is it?

Where is it?

Great. See you then. Bye!

Social Science

HOME LEADERS SUPPORT US ABOUT US PRESS

THE DUKE OF EDINBURGH'S AWARD

There are three Duke of Edinburgh's Awards

BRONZE SILVER GOLD

HELP & ACCESSIBILITY STATEMENTS | PRIVACY AND DISCLAIMER | SITE MAP | © THE DUKE OF EDINBURGH'S AWARD 2010 | PRINT THIS PAGE

1  **Read and number the photos.**

Children of 14 and over can do the Duke of Edinburgh's **Award**. A teacher helps them. It takes about six months to do an award.

You have to do something from each of these sections:

1 Physical: getting better at a sport or dancing

2 Volunteering: helping other people or animals

3 Skills: learning how to do something new

4 Expedition: going on a two-day trip and staying one night in a tent

2 Read and write the names of the sections from 1.

Planning for a Bronze award

(1) <u>Volunteering</u> : You can help old people, children, people with **special needs**, animals or people who live on the streets. You can help with gardening, shopping, cooking, cleaning or talking to people who don't have friends or family. You must do this for three months.

(2) _____ : What are your hobbies? You can do **photography**, computer skills, painting, singing, playing a musical instrument, **sewing**, **knitting**, making things or being a DJ! It doesn't matter what you do, the important thing is to learn something new. You do this section for three months.

(3) _____ : What sport do you like doing? Choose your favourite and do something new in it for three months. You can do swimming, football, basketball, climbing, tennis or dancing. You can do anything! The idea is to get fitter and better at it.

(4)_____ : You do this with four to seven other people. You can go **sailing**, walking, cycling, horse riding or climbing. You plan the two-day **trip**; what you're going to eat and where you're going to go, and you camp for one night in a tent. It's a great adventure!

3 Read again and complete.

Sections	Volunteering	Skills	Physical	Expedition
Three things you can do	1 <u>helping children</u> 2 _____ 3 _____	1 _____ 2 _____ 3 _____	1 _____ 2 _____ 3 _____	1 _____ 2 _____ 3 _____
How long does it take?	three months			

4 Your project! Complete the plan for you and write.

	do a sport	help people	learn something new
What are you going to do?	football	shopping for grandma	
When are you going to start?	Monday	tomorrow	

I'm going to do two things. I'm going to learn to play football better. I'm going to start on Monday.

I'm going to help people, too. I'm going to do the shopping for my grandma. I'm going to start tomorrow!

Review 4

1 Look, circle and write.

knock over   ~~jump on~~   close   sit on   clean   use
~~the sofa~~   the cushion   the phone   the rug   the lamp   the curtains

1 The cat (is) / are going to ___jump on the sofa___ .

2 Grandpa is / are going to _____ .

3 The girl is / are going to _____ .

4 The boy and the dog is / are going to _____ .

5 Mum is / are going to _____ .

6 Dad is / are going to _____ .

2 What about you? Choose and write. Then answer.

rock climbing   ~~ice skating~~   cycling   skateboarding

1 Do you like ___ice skating___ ?
___Yes, I do. / No, I don't.___

3 Do you want to go _____ ?
_____

2 Are you good at _____ ?
_____

4 Are you happy when you're _____ ?
_____

3 Listen and match. Then ask and answer. •))

   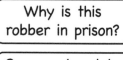

Why is this robber in prison?

Because he stole some valuable paintings.

4 Listen and chant. •))

These three trees are thin and those three trees are thick.

Where's the girl?

She's at the beach.

What time is it?

It's quarter to two.

What's she going to do?

She's going to go surfing.

Its number 2.

That's right!

The Voyages of Sindbad the Sailor

1 **Read and listen.** •))

PENGUIN READERS

The Voyages of Sindbad the Sailor

I am Sindbad the **sailor**. This is the story of my sixth **voyage**. 'I'm going to make one last voyage,' I thought.

It was a long and **dangerous** voyage. It was very windy. We were lost. The **captain** pointed to a mountain in front of us.

'Can you see that mountain?' the captain shouted. 'There is a cave at its foot. The sea is taking our **ship** into it. I cannot stop it now. When a man goes in there, he dies!'

The sailors tried to sail the ship out of the fast water but it was impossible. The mountain came nearer and nearer. Suddenly the water carried our ship into the cave. Inside, the ship hit the walls and broke. There were men and **wood** everywhere in the water.

'Where are you?' I called.

I listened but there was no answer. 'I can't help my friends, I thought. The water was fast and it carried me through the cave on some wood from the ship.

My journey through those black caves was very long. I was tired and **afraid**. I fell asleep.

When I woke up, I heard shouts. I opened my eyes and looked around me. I was next to a great river. People looked down on me. The noise came from them. 'Who are you?' I asked. 'Can you help me?'

They answered me, 'You are in the country of the great king of Serendip.'

I was happy then because I knew about this great king and his country. I knew he was kind to people.

'These mountains are dangerous. How did you come here?'

I told them how our ship went into the cave near the sea and broke on the walls.

I cried. 'My friends are dead. I was afraid on that long and dangerous journey!'

A man said, 'You must tell this story to the king. Let's go now.'

They brought a horse for me and we left the river. After three days we arrived at the king's city.

The king liked the story of my great adventure. He wanted to hear more stories. He was kind. He gave me rooms and the best clothes and food and other good things. He sent for me day after day and I told him the story of all my voyages.

One day I heard about a ship.

'This ship is going to my city,' I said. 'Can I go home now?'

'Yes, go,' said the king. 'Here is a letter for your king and many rich things for you and him.'

'Thank you,' I answered.

I had a good voyage home and I took the presents to the king. Then I went back to my house and met my friends again.

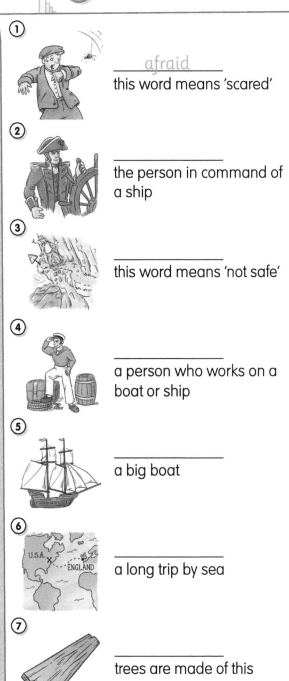

2 Find and write.

1. _____afraid_____
   this word means 'scared'

2. _____
   the person in command of a ship

3. _____
   this word means 'not safe'

4. _____
   a person who works on a boat or ship

5. _____
   a big boat

6. _____
   a long trip by sea

7. _____
   trees are made of this

1 Listen and say. Then listen and read. 🔊

 hot air balloon

 disappear

 explain

 return

1. Where's Jack?

I don't know. He was here at breakfast and then he disappeared!

2. Is he waiting outside?

No, I can't see him.

This is Mr Falcon. I explained that we need to return home. He's got a hot air balloon we can use.

3. There he is!

Who's that with him?

4. That's wonderful. I can fly a hot air balloon!

5. Off we go!

Toto likes the hot air balloon!

6. Look at the fields and that big forest over there.

Oscar is enjoying the trip!

7. Hooray! We're home.

Thank you, Aunt Sophie. That was a great adventure.

2 Let's learn! Read.

Remember!

He likes the balloon.	Does he like the balloon?	He doesn't like the balloon.
He's waiting.	Is he waiting?	He isn't waiting.
He was here.	Was he here?	He wasn't here.
He explained.	Did he explain?	He didn't explain.

3 Read the story again and match.

1 They're looking for Jack. _Picture 2_

2 They're looking at the fields. _____

3 Kelly's thanking her aunt. _____

4 They're waving goodbye to Mr Falcon. _____

4 Listen and tick the correct pictures. Then say. •))

Every day she gets up at quarter past six.

1
 a
 b ✔

2
 a
 b

3
 a
 b

4
 a
 b

5 Look and match. Then say.

1 return — c home safely
2 open   a to Sally on the phone
3 email   b the party invitation
4 talk   d Toto on the News
5 watch   e his friends

What did they do?   *They returned home safely.*

9b I lost my paddle!

1 Listen and say. Then listen and read. •))

 horse riding  camping canoeing paddle restaurant Chinese

Beth: Whose photos are these?

Kit: They're Jack and Kelly's. Look – they're in a hot air balloon.

Beth: I flew to America last year but I didn't fly in a hot air balloon. I went by plane.

Kit: Here's Kelly at that farm. She went horse riding there. Did you go horse riding last summer?

Beth: Yes, I did. I loved it!

Kit: I don't know when they took this photo. It's a tent in the mountains.

Beth: Perhaps they went camping.

Kit: I slept in a tent at school camp. It was great.

Beth: Look at this photo. Jack is canoeing.

Kit: I went canoeing once but I was terrible. I lost my paddle!

Beth: Here they're in a Chinese restaurant. I ate Chinese food at a restaurant in London.

Kit: Did you like it?

Beth: Yes, I did.

2 Read the story again and tick.

	Jack	Kelly	Kit	Beth
1 Who flew in a hot air balloon?	✔	✔	___	___
2 Who flew in a plane?	___	___	___	___
3 Who went horse riding?	___	___	___	___
4 Who went to school camp?	___	___	___	___
5 Who lost a paddle?	___	___	___	___
6 Who ate Chinese food?	___	___	___	___

3 Let's learn! Read.

Remember!

I flew in a hot air balloon.   I didn't fly in a plane.
Did you fly in a helicopter?   Yes, I did./No, I didn't.

4 Complete with a tick or cross. Then ask and answer.

go horse riding   go canoeing   fly in a plane   see a hot air balloon
eat Chinese food   sleep in a tent

Last summer

You						
Your friend						

Did you fly in a plane last summer?

No, I didn't but I went horse riding.

5 Look at 4 and write.

1 Last summer I _went horse riding_ .

2 I didn't _____ .

3 Last summer my friend _____ .

4 My friend didn't _____ .

6 Listen, choose and write. Then sing. •))

slept   ~~had~~   swam   climbed   went   met

Last summer I (1) __had__ a lovely time.
I (2) _____ camping with some friends of mine.
We rode our bikes and we (3) _____ a tree.
We played on the beach and we (4) _____ in the sea.
We (5) _____ in a tent and we paddled a canoe.
We (6) _____ lots of people and made new friends, too!

All our friends are going to be there.

1 Listen and say. Then listen and read. •))

 top
 collar
 brush
 forget
 smart

Jack: I'm so excited. It's the picnic tomorrow.

Kelly: Is Beth going to go?

Jack: Yes, all our friends are going to be there! I can't wait to see them and tell them about our adventures.

Kelly: Do we have to take anything?

Jack: Aunt Sophie is going to buy some picnic food this afternoon.

Kelly: What are you going to wear?

Jack: I'm going to wear my new T-shirt and jeans. What about you?

Kelly: I'm not sure. Shall I wear my red dress or my orange top and blue skirt?

Jack: I like the orange top best.

Dr Wild: Yes, wear your orange top and blue skirt, Kelly.

Kelly: OK.

Dr Wild: We mustn't forget Oscar. Jack, are you going to brush him?

Jack: Yes, I am.

Dr Wild: I can buy him a new collar when I go to the supermarket.

Kelly: Oh thank you, Aunt Sophie. He's going to be the smartest cat in the world!

2 Let's learn! Read.

I'm going to go to a party!

Remember!
Jack is going to wear his new T-shirt.
Kelly isn't going to wear her red dress.
Is Oscar going to wear a new collar? Yes, he is.

3 Read the story again and answer.

1 Are their friends going to be at the picnic?
Yes, they are.

2 Is Jack going to buy the food? _____

3 Is Kelly going to wear her red dress?
_____

4 Is Kelly going to brush Oscar? _____

5 Are they going to buy Oscar a new brush?
_____

6 Is Oscar going to be the smartest cat in the world? _____

4 Look, choose and say.

chase a cat   take a photo   have a picnic   read a newspaper   ~~feed the ducks~~   play tennis

The girl is going to feed the ducks.

5 Think and write with Dr Wild.

go to school
visit your grandma
go to the cinema
go swimming
play football
play with your friends
tidy your room
watch TV
do your homework

Write what you are and aren't going to do tomorrow.

I'm going to go to school.
I'm not going to visit my
grandma.
_____
_____
_____

You need to take a camera.

1 Look at the pictures and say.

> Picture 1: It's an elephant.

Dear Kelly and Jack,

Thank you very much for rescuing Toto. Your aunt told me how helpful you were. We're very happy that he's back at the zoo. He's very happy, too!

I'm in South Africa on holiday. It's a very beautiful country. Yesterday I drove through Kruger National Park and saw lots of amazing animals — hippos, zebras, giraffes, elephants, lions and a rhino. They live in the wild and you have to look carefully to see them. Tomorrow is my last day and I want to go on a trip in a hot air balloon. I hope I don't fall out! See you back in England.

Love from Sally

Miss K and Mr J Wild

8 Tower Street

Bristol, BR8 1JP

2 Read and tick the animals Sally saw.

3 Read again and answer.

1 Who did Sally talk to? _____Dr Wild_____

2 Where is Toto? _____

3 Where is Sally? _____

4 Do the giraffes live in the zoo?

_____

5 What does Sally want to do tomorrow?

_____

Writing class: AB, page 106

4 Listen and match. •))

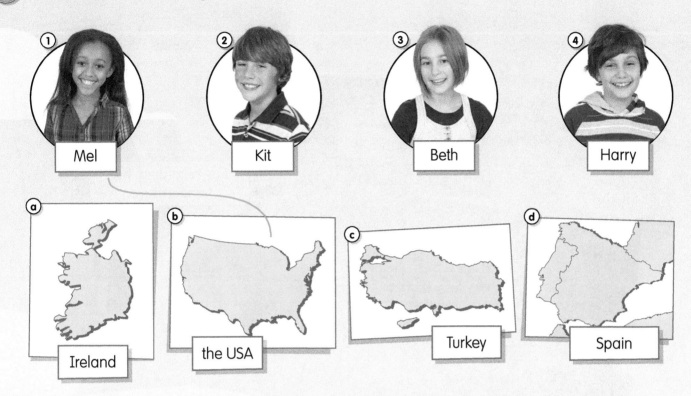

① Mel ② Kit ③ Beth ④ Harry

a Ireland
b the USA
c Turkey
d Spain

5 Listen again and complete. •))

Where is he/she going?	How long is the trip?	What does he/she need to take?
1 the USA / England	three weeks	a camera
2 Ukraine / Turkey		
3 Spain / Argentina		
4 Ireland / Australia		

6 Choose ideas from 5 and write. Then act it out.

I'm so excited. We're going to _____ tomorrow.

Yes, it is.

_____ .

That's a good idea. Thank you.

That's fantastic. Is this your first visit?

How long are you going for?

It's _____ . You need to take _____ .

the Arctic

North Pole

scientist

I'm recording the temperature.

dark

light

South Pole

the Antarctic

1 **Guess and tick or cross.**

	polar bear	walrus	seal	fox	whale	penguin
the Arctic	✔					
the Antarctic	✘					

2 **Read and check.**

The Arctic and Antarctic are the coldest places on Earth. There's lots of snow and ice and it's always cold. In summer it's light all day and all night. In winter it's dark all the time.

The Arctic is an exciting place. There are small towns where people live. Whales, walruses, seals, foxes and polar bears live near the North Pole. In winter some animals, such as foxes, change colour. They change from brown to white so they can hide in the snow from other animals.

In the Antarctic there are no plants because it's too cold. It's colder than the Arctic and on July 21st 1983 the temperature was minus 89°C. This is the lowest temperature ever recorded. It's the coldest, windiest and driest continent on the planet. The Antarctic has about 90% of the world's ice.

There aren't many people in the Antarctic. Scientists visit the Research Stations and you can go there on holiday. It's beautiful and there's lots to see. There aren't any polar bears, foxes or walruses but there are whales and seals and 17 different kinds of penguin. It's an amazing place.

3 **Read again and write Arctic or Antarctic.**

1 The South Pole is in the middle of this continent.
   Antarctic

2 It's the windiest place in the world.
   _____

3 Animals change colour in winter.
   _____

4 Penguins live here._____

5 You can see polar bears and walruses here.
   _____

6 It has the coldest temperature ever recorded.
   _____

7 People live here. _____

8 Scientists visit here to do research.
   _____

4 **Your project!** Design and make a poster about your country for a visitor.

Ireland is a small island. There are lots of hills and rivers in Ireland. It's very green because it rains a lot. You can see lots of birds and farm animals. There are cows, sheep and horses in the fields. It's very pretty.

Goodbye!

1 **Listen and read. Then ask and answer.** •))

What was your favourite part of the story?

I liked _____.

 **Sing.**

We learnt lots of new things
And made some new friends, too.
We had parties and meals and trips.
There were so many things to do!

What a great adventure!
We had so much fun!
We had good times, happy times, funny times.
Now our work is done!

We were all together
In good times and in bad.
We laughed and sang and worked and played.
What a good time we had!

What a great adventure!
We had so much fun!
We had good times, happy times, funny times.
Now our work is done!

1 **Read and write. Then match.**

 a
 b
 c 1

 d
 e
 f

1 The children __are arriving__ (arrive) at the theatre.

2 The race _____ (start).

3 They _____ (watch) a DVD about London.

4 The teacher _____ (explain) where polar bears live.

5 The class _____ (return) from the school trip.

6 The children _____ (have) an Art lesson.

2 **Look, choose and write. Use need/needs.**

have ~~buy~~ take look

 ①
 ②
 ③
 ④

1 She ___needs to buy___ some new shoes.

2 He _____ his umbrella.

3 He _____ a shower.

4 They _____ at the map.

3 **What about you? Read and circle. Then answer.**

1 Do you live / lived near your school?

_____

2 Is / Are there a computer in your classroom?

_____

3 Did you eat / ate a sandwich for lunch today?

_____

4 Did you go / went swimming yesterday?

_____

4 **Listen and chant.** •))

Kit with his kite hoped to hop but it made him mad.

5 **Play the game.**

The Yazoo Show

Child 1: What shall we do today?

Child 2: I don't know. What's the weather like?

Child 3: There are big black clouds in the sky and it's raining now!

Child 4: It's very windy, too.

Child 5: I like storms!

Child 6: Me, too, but my cat doesn't!

Child 1: I love your cat. He's so funny.

All sing: He's a little bit lazy. (Unit 6b)

Child 2: What did you do yesterday? Did you do anything exciting?

Child 3: Well, we had a good day yesterday.

Child 4: But it wasn't very exciting.

Child 5: We went to school.

Child 6: I helped my parents.

All sing: Yesterday I stayed at home. (Unit 2b)

Child 1: I played with my old toys. Look – this is my old train. I loved this when I was younger. It was my favourite toy.

Child 2: Look! Can you see what I can see?

Child 3: It's a train!

Child 4: Where did it come from?

Child 5: It came with the storm!

Child 6: Look – there's a train driver. She's coming here.

Train driver: Come with me. We're going on an adventure!

Child 4: It isn't raining now!

Child 5: Where are we going?

Train driver: It's a surprise. Follow me!

Child 1: Do we need tickets?

Train driver: Don't worry. I've got them!

All sing: We're travelling on the train. (Unit 4b)

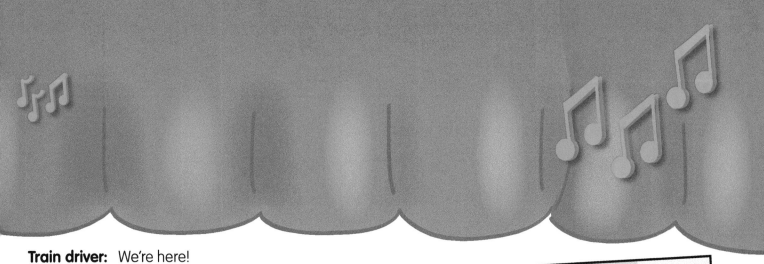

Train driver:	We're here!
Child 2:	Where are we?
Child 3:	I can see girls and women wearing long dresses.
Child 4:	That little boy is wearing a dress, too!
Child 5:	We're in the past!
Train driver:	Yes, we're in London in the 17th century!
Child 6:	Look! There's the Tower of London.
Child 1:	I can smell something strange.
Child 2:	Fire!
Child 3:	It's the Great Fire of London!
Train driver:	Quick! Get on the train again.
All sing:	We learnt lots of new things. (Goodbye!)

[Train driver exits quietly while the other children are not looking.]

Child 4:	Home again.
Child 5:	Thank you. That was a wonderful adventure.
Child 6:	Where's the train driver?
Child 1:	She's not here!
Child 2:	Did that really happen? Did we really go on a train and visit the past?
Child 3:	I don't know. I'm confused!
Child 4:	But we had great fun.
All children:	Yes, we did!
All sing:	Did you have a good day yesterday? (Unit 3b)

Teacher's Day

1 **Listen and say. Then listen and read.** •))

Ancient Greece

wax

stick

wrestling

hit

strict

What's your teacher called? Is your teacher a man or a woman? How many teachers are there in your school?

In Ancient Greece the teachers were all men. There weren't any women teachers. There were grammar teachers, music teachers and PE teachers. They didn't have blackboards or books. They wrote lessons for the children on wood. There was wax on the wood. They didn't have pens, they had sticks. They taught reading, writing, thinking and music. In the afternoons the PE teachers taught wrestling!

Much later, in the 18th century, there were women and men teachers. The teachers were very strict then and they sometimes hit the children with sticks.

In the 19th century the famous English author Charles Dickens wrote about a very strict teacher in his book *Hard Times*. The teacher's name was Mr Gradgrind. He didn't like children thinking and having ideas. He said they must only learn facts. Teachers wrote on blackboards at the front of the class.

Today there are books, pens, computers and games in our schools. Men and women can be teachers. In their classrooms they sometimes have blackboards like in the 1800s but now they have whiteboards as well. Our teachers are sometimes strict but they're kind, too, and they like children thinking and having lots of ideas!

2 **Read again and write True or False.**

1 There were men and women teachers in Ancient Greece. __False__
2 Teachers wrote on wood in Ancient Greece. _____
3 PE teachers taught wrestling in the afternoons in Ancient Greece. _____
4 In the 18th century the teachers sometimes hit the children. _____
5 Charles Dickens was a famous English teacher. _____
6 Mr Gradgrind was a kind teacher. _____

3 Listen and circle. •))

1 Mrs Baker teaches	**a** (English.)	**b** Maths.	**c** Science.
2 Her favourite food is	**a** chicken sandwiches.	**b** chicken and salad.	**c** chicken and chips.
3 She wants to go to	**a** England.	**b** Russia.	**c** India.
4 She's got a	**a** white cat.	**b** big cat.	**c** white dog.
5 Her favourite sport is	**a** football.	**b** walking.	**c** swimming.
6 Her favourite clothes are	**a** red skirt/black sweater.	**b** red sweater/black skirt.	**c** red dress/black shoes.

4 Guess about your teacher. Then ask and write.

	My guess	My teacher's answer
What's your favourite food?		
Where in the world do you want to go?		
Have you got any pets?		
What's your favourite sport?		
What are your favourite clothes?		

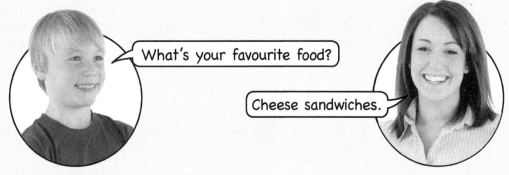

5 Listen and number. Then sing. •))

☐ You teach us what is wrong and right.

☐ And lots of games to play.

☐ You teach us words to say.

1 You teach us how to think and write.

☐ And we have lots of fun as well.

☐ Teacher, we love you!

☐ You teach us how to read and spell.

☐ You teach us what to do.

Valentine's Day

1 **Listen and say.** 🔊

message

rose

violet

heart

2 **Guess and circle. Then read and check.**

1 When is Valentine's Day?   February 14th / May 1st / July 4th

2 How old is Valentine's Day?   100 years old / 300 years old / 600 years old

3 What do people send on Valentine's Day?   money / cards / clothes

4 What do people give on Valentine's Day?   eggs / birds / flowers

February 14th is a special day. It's Valentine's Day. It's a day to tell somebody that you love them. This tradition started in Europe more than 600 years ago. About 200 years ago people started sending Valentine's cards.
The cards have messages of friendship and love. Sometimes the cards don't say who they're from. It's a secret and the person never knows who sent the card. Today people send cards or give presents, such as flowers and chocolates, on Valentine's Day.

3 **Listen to the traditional Valentine's messages and circle.** 🔊

①
(1) Roses / Tomatoes are red,
(2) Oceans / Violets are blue.
(3) Sugar / Honey is sweet
And so are you.

②
My love is like a (4) carrot / cabbage.
Cut up into (5) two / three.
The (6) leaves / flowers I give to others,
The (7) eyes / heart I give to you.

4 **Read and tick the Valentine's Day messages.**

(1) My best friend is the one who brings out the best in me. ✔

(2) I love you. Be my Valentine. xxx

(3) Happy Easter

(6) I GIVE YOU MY HEART. BE MINE.

(4) Happy Birthday to you

(5) HAPPY VALENTINE'S DAY

(7) Merry Christmas

5 **Choose a message and make a Valentine's card for your friend.**

Happy Valentine's Day

I love you

6 **Read and learn the poem.**

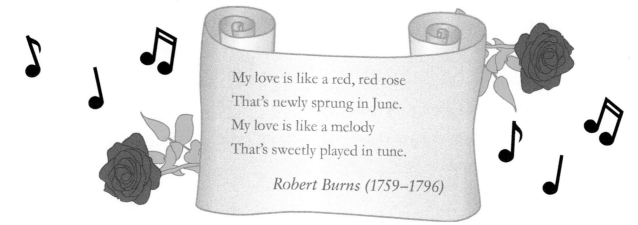

My love is like a red, red rose
That's newly sprung in June.
My love is like a melody
That's sweetly played in tune.

Robert Burns (1759–1796)

The Queen's Birthday

1 **Listen and say. Then listen and read.** •)

gun salute   midday   parade

The Queen

The kings and queens of the United Kingdom celebrate two birthdays every year. Queen Elizabeth II was born on April 21st 1926. This is her real birthday. She also has an official birthday on a Saturday in June.

On April 21st the Queen spends a quiet day with her family and friends. At midday there are gun salutes in London – a 41-gun salute in Hyde Park and a 62-gun salute in the Tower of London.

A 21-gun salute

On special birthdays they play the National Anthem on the radio. There aren't any big celebrations in April.

The main celebrations are in June because the weather is better than in April. On her official birthday the Queen and her family watch soldiers in a parade called the Trooping of the Colour. Thousands of people from around the world watch the Birthday Parade with her. This tradition started in 1748. It's the biggest royal celebration of the year in Britain.

The Trooping of the Colour

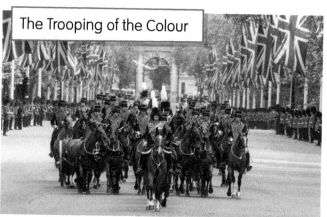

2 **Read again and write.**

1 The Queen was born in ___April___ .

2 The Queen's official birthday is in _____ .

3 On the Queen's real birthday there are gun salutes in _____ .

4 The Trooping of the Colour for the King or Queen's birthday started in _____ .

5 The Birthday Parade is the biggest _____ .

3 **Listen and circle.** 🔊

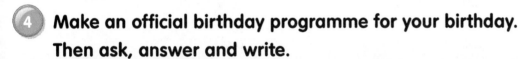

1 It's June 12th / June 14th.

2 At twenty to eleven the Queen leaves
the Tower of London / Buckingham Palace.

3 The parade starts at
eleven o'clock / half past eleven.

4 The foot soldiers and the soldiers on horses follow
the Queen / the bands.

5 The parade lasts about an hour / two hours.

6 The planes fly past Buckingham Palace at
half past twelve / one o'clock.

4 **Make an official birthday programme for your birthday.**
Then ask, answer and write.

 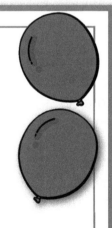

My official birthday is on December 1st.

On my birthday I want to have a snow party in the forest.
I'm going to invite my friends. We're going to make a
snowman. Then we're going to go for a ride on a dog sled.
Afterwards we're going to cook sausages in a tent.

When's your official birthday? _____

What kind of celebration are you going to have? _____

Where's it going to be? _____

Who are you going to invite? _____

What are you going to do? _____

Word list

Welcome
detective
missing

1a Where's Toto?
niece
nephew
clever
lazy
friendly
helpful

1b We're getting ready!
laptop
binoculars
compass
can opener
torch
diary
need

1c Dr Wild drives well.
carefully
badly
well
slowly
quietly
happily
quickly

Music: Music around the world
bagpipes
blow
loud
tango
opera
bell
polonaise
composer
didgeridoo

2a There was a storm.
storm
thunder and lightning
worried
windy
behind
in front of

2b We landed on a beach.
aquarium
town hall
police station
pet shop
museum
café
follow

2c Did you talk to them?
moustache
beard
face
blond
thin
wavy
notice

Geography: Hurricanes
hurricane
flood
tornado
natural disaster
last
cause
produce
travel
destroy

Story Time 1: Robinson Crusoe
tools
knife
journey
land
island
cave
strange
footprint

3a Magnus and Claudia had an accident!
farm
cow
grass
owl
pond
bull

3b Did they find Toto?
scared
confused
nervous
unhappy

3c Claudia and Magnus had colds.
cold
headache
sore throat
earache
stomachache
well
ill

Technology: Communication
newspaper
e-book reader
letter
paper
clay
size
machine
communicate
appear
weigh

4a They went through the town.
train station
road
market
castle
bridge
hotel

4b How much were the tickets?
carriage
seat
money
luggage
search
look after

4c There aren't many peas.
stew
rice
cabbage
steak
peas

Geography: Map reading
art gallery
church
tower
Big Wheel
palace
crown
cathedral

Story Time 2: Alice in Wonderland
hare
place
wine
tea
polite
wide
angrily

5a I can hear Claudia's voice.
voice
ribbon
neck
toes
elbow
knees
tummy

5b Is it yours?
scarf
glove
jacket
belt
trainers
tie
rescue

5c You don't have to shout!
arrive
leave
start
lose
bring
finish

History: Clothes through the ages
eleventh – 11th
twelfth – 12th
thirteenth – 13th
fourteenth – 14th
fifteenth – 15th
sixteenth – 16th
seventeenth – 17th
eighteenth – 18th
nineteenth – 19th

twentieth – 20th
twenty-first – 21st
breeches
cap
tunic
apron
fashion
school uniform
casual

6a The red van is better!
van
motorbike
fire engine
scooter
helicopter

6b They're the silliest people in the world!
runner
catch
silly
heavy
noisy
light

6c Oscar has got the softest bed!
tobogganing
rich
cheap
dark
soft
hard
easy

Science: Planets
rock
ring
gas
star
ice
furthest

Story Time 3: The Prince and the Pauper
soldier
beggar
servant
pauper
beg
poor

7a I want to join in.
fancy dress
costume
alien
superhero
pop star
join in

7b He likes tobogganing!
ice skating
surfing
skateboarding
rock climbing
cycling
fishing

7c What shall we do?
use
escape
reach
borrow
hold

PE: Sporting legends
goal
world record
gold medal
score
compete
Olympic

8a I'm going to phone the police!
lamp
curtain
rug
sofa
cushion
prison
knock over

8b Are they going to come home now?
picnic
invitation
banner
plan
send

8c Why did they want Toto?
robber
jewellery
painting
diamond
steal
rare
valuable

Social Science: Duke of Edinburgh's Award
award
physical
volunteering
skills
expedition
special needs
photography
sewing
knitting
sailing
trip

Story Time 4: The Voyages of Sindbad the Sailor
sailor
voyage
dangerous
captain
ship
wood
afraid

9a Oscar is enjoying the trip!
hot air balloon
disappear
explain
return

9b I lost my paddle!
horse riding
camping
canoeing
paddle
restaurant
Chinese

9c All our friends are going to be there.
top
collar
brush
forget
smart

Geography: The Arctic and Antarctic
the Arctic
the Antarctic
North Pole
South Pole
scientist
polar bear
walrus
seal
light
dark

Teacher's Day
Ancient Greece
wax
stick
wrestling
hit
strict

Valentine's Day
message
rose
violet
heart

The Queen's Birthday
gun salute
midday
parade

Irregular verbs

Base Form	Simple Past	Past Participle	Base Form	Simple Past	Past Participle
be	was/were	been	lose	lost	lost
begin	began	begun	make	made	made
bring	brought	brought	meet	met	met
buy	bought	bought	put	put	put
catch	caught	caught	read	read	read
come	came	come	ride	rode	ridden
cut	cut	cut	ring	rang	rung
do	did	done	run	ran	run
draw	drew	drawn	say	said	said
drink	drank	drunk	see	saw	seen
drive	drove	driven	sell	sold	sold
eat	ate	eaten	send	sent	sent
fall	fell	fallen	sing	sang	sung
feed	fed	fed	sit	sat	sat
feel	felt	felt	sleep	slept	slept
fight	fought	fought	speak	spoke	spoken
find	found	found	stand	stood	stood
fly	flew	flown	steal	stole	stolen
get	got	got	swim	swam	swum
give	gave	given	take	took	taken
go	went	gone	tell	told	told
grow	grew	grown	think	thought	thought
hear	heard	heard	throw	threw	thrown
hide	hid	hidden	understand	understood	understood
hit	hit	hit	wake up	woke up	woken up
hold	held	held	wear	wore	worn
know	knew	known	write	wrote	written
learn	learnt	learnt			
leave	left	left			

Pearson Education Limited
Edinburgh Gate
Harlow
Essex CM20 2JE
England
and Associated Companies throughout the world.

www.pearsonlongman.com

First published 2011
This impression 2022
ISBN: 978-1-4082-4986-4
Set in VagRounded Infant
Printed and bound by CPI Group (UK) Ltd, Croydon, CR0 4YY

Acknowledgements
The publisher would like to thank the following for their kind permission to reproduce their photographs:

(Key: b-bottom; c-centre; l-left; r-right; t-top)

Alamy Images: ACE STOCK LIMITED 80bl, amana images inc. 120, Art Directors & TRIP 38/7, Alan Keith Beastall 80tl, Ben Molyneux Travel Photography 46 (e), Tibor Bognar 14br, chrisstockphoto 80tr, Colin Palmer Photography 46 (d), imagebroker 17b, 22t, Darrin Jenkins 38/3, Kuttig - People 48, Johannes Leber 104tl, Neil McAllister 49r, mediablitzimages (uk) Limited 84/2, PCL 14tl, SHOUT 60/3, Steve Allen Travel Photography 14bl, CountrySideCollection – Homer Sykes 96bl, Rob Walls 96tr; **Corbis:** Radius Images 80br; **Education Photos:** John Walmsley 60/1; **Fotolia.com:** allievn 108/4, Lance Bellers 46 (c), Peter Betts 108/3, Borodaev 39br, Sebastian Crocker 39bl, Vladimir Liverts 39tr, nyasha 39bc; **Getty Images:** 122bl, Shaun Botterill 86tr, Pando Hall 123r, Alexander Hassenstein 87, Harry How 86bl, Anwar Hussein 122r, Samir Hussein 123l, Bellurget Jean Louis 38/6, Jonathan Morgan 38/5, National Geographic / Mike Theiss 24br, Joern Pollex 86tl, Science Faction 104bl, John Stillwell 122tl, Peter Teller 96tl, US Coast Guard / Kyle Niemi 24tr; **iStockphoto:** blackwaterimages 119r; **Pearson Education Ltd:** 65, Jon Barlow 8, 9, 12, 18, 22c, 22b, 23t, 32, 42, 46 (b), 58, 61t, 66, 71t, 79l, 81t, 84t, 90, 109t, 112-113t, Trevor Clifford 7, 13, 17c, 19, 21, 23b, 31, 37, 41, 47, 50, 55, 59, 61b, 62, 67, 71b, 79r, 81b, 85, 91, 95, 103, 105, 107, 109b, 112b, 119l; **Pearson Education Ltd:** Digital Stock 108/2, Digital Vision 108/5, Photodisc 39tl, Photodisc / Alan D. Carey 108/7, Photodisc / Getty Images 24bl, Photodisc / Jack Hollingsworth Photography 108/1, Photodisc / StockTrek 24tl; **Photolibrary.com:** Cusp 38/1, Fancy 38/4, Moodboard 38/2; **PunchStock:** Digital Vision 96br; **Reuters:** Wolfgang Rattay 86br; **Shutterstock.com:** Mihai Blanaru 14bc, Bogdan Postelnicu 46 (a), Stanislaw Tokarski 14tr; **Thinkstock:** 49l, 60/2, 60/4, 84/1, 104br, Digital Vision 108/6, Hemera 84/4, 94, 104tr, 111l, Hemera 84/4, 94, 104tr, 111l, Hemera Technologies 84/3, iStockphoto 84/5, Medioimages / Photodisc 111r, Stockbyte 84/6, 84/7

All other images © Pearson Education

Every effort has been made to trace the copyright holders and we apologise in advance for any unintentional omissions. We would be pleased to insert the appropriate acknowledgement in any subsequent edition of this publication.

Illustrated by Diego Diaz/Lemonade (Main character artwork); Sean Longcroft (Incidental and scene artwork); Stephanie Strickland (Word Icons); Jurgen Zewie/Debut Art (3D/Realistic artwork); Vasili Zorin/Debut Art (Story artwork); Dan Chernett